THE HISTORY OF
THE SCALA CINEMA
PRESTATYN

Fred Hobbs

Chairman of the Prestatyn Local History Club

&

The Friends of the Scala

a

publication

Fred Hobbs

THE HISTORY OF THE SCALA CINEMA PRESTATYN

© 2009 Fred Hobbs

Friends of the Scala
(Reg. Charity No 1116865)
ISBN 978-1-902964-09-6

Published by Middleview

an imprint of Avid Publications
Middleview, New Road,
GWESPYR
Flintshire. U.K
CH8 9LS
Tel : (44) 01745 886769
e-mail: info@AvidPublications.co.uk

Other publications available from Avid / Middleview are detailed
at the rear of this book

Every effort has been made by the author and the Friends of the Scala to trace the owners of any
copyright material used in this book; should any material have been included inadvertently
without the permission of the owner of the copyright we apologise unreservedly and
acknowledgement will made in any future edition. Some of the images here are very old and
rare. They are taken from newsprint and as such do not offer the best reproduction. We hope the
reader will forgive the graininess and concentrate instead on the hard work and dedication given
by Fred Hobbs and the Friends of the Scala to produce this book.

To Sonia

CONTENTS

List of Sponsers   6

Chapter 1   Introduction   9

Chapter 2   Introduction of Culture to Prestatyn   21

Chapter 3   The Coming of the Picture House   23

Chapter 4   Saronie and the Cinema   25

Chapter 5   The Scala is very well used   46

Chapter 6   Looking back

            - Seventeen years with the Saronies   77

            Mrs Vivien Hughes-Davies

Chapter 7   From start to finish

            - The show must go on   83

            Sandra Pitt - (Chair: Friends of the Scala)

INDIVIDUAL SPONSORS

Rhiannon Hughes Prestatyn
Connie Brierly Victoria Road F O S Prestatyn
Betty Peters F.O.S Prestatyn
Dave and Moira Turner Grosvenor Road F.O.S Prestatyn
Glenys A Wood F O S Prestatyn
Melanie J Pitt Ffordd Parc Bodnant F O S Prestatyn Ex Staff
Sian Barker Heather Crescent F O S Prestatyn
Luke Gordon Crozier Ffordd Parc Bodnant Prestatyn
Lucy Davies Ffordd Idwal Prestatyn
Sam Davies Ffordd Idwal Prestatyn
Jack Davies Llangefni Angelsey
Daniel Davies Ffordd Idwal Prestatyn
Duncan Bradshaw Wheatcroft Green Lanes Prestatyn
Jessica Crozier Ffordd Parc Bodnant Prestatyn
Colin Pitt Victoria Road Prestatyn
Jamie Pitt Blaenau Ffestiniog
Zoe Pitt Blaenau Ffestiniog
Christopher Pitt Oakville Ave Rhyl
Gavin and Gwen Pitt Rhyl
Gary Bourne's Club Teen Prestatyn
Marie Bourne Lon Eirlys Prestatyn
Natashia Bourne Lon Eirlys Prestatyn
Felix Bourne Lon Eirlys Prestatyn
Mrs Joyce Bezodis Prestatyn
Murial Curno Hawarden Scala staff 2009
Sam Clarke Trevor Ave Rhuddlan Scala staff 2009
Natalie Graham-Hammond Pendyffryn Rd Rhyl Scala Staff 2009

Cloe Barker Heather Crescent Prestatyn
Jamine Barker Heather Crescent Prestatyn
Hayley Marie Owens Melyd Ave Scala Staff 2009
Derek & Ann Williams Princess Ave Prestatyn
Andrew Prichard Llys Gwylan Rhyl
Jenny & Gerald Orchard Prestatyn
Janet & Geoffrey Groves Hopley London
Sherry Edwards Prestatyn
Chris Ruane MP Rhyl
G Roberts Prestatyn
Jo & Chris Groves Grosvenor Rd. Prestatyn
Mrs Phyllis Loveland Prestatyn
Mrs Kay Northan Prestatyn
Mr Ray Harris Fforddisa Prestatyn
Joan & Stan Baker Linden Walk Prestatyn
Susan Christou Nant Drive Prestatyn
Dr Julian Christou. Hawaii, United States (formally of Prestatyn)
Mr A. K. Pal Plastirion Ave Prestatyn
Ron & Mavis Taylor Prestatyn
Pauline Bell Prestatyn
Doctor Douglas MacLeod Prestatyn
Mrs Joan Steel Ffordd Pendyfryn Prestatyn
Joan Bains Plas Gorffwysfa Prestatyn
Betty Ward The Mall, Prestatyn
Frank & Lilian Bailey Oldgate Road Vice Chair F.O.S. Prestatyn
Andy & Julie Owens & The Girls Tan-Y-Felin, Greenfield
Andrew & Kate Bailey & The Boys 'Cae Haf' Northop Hall.
Chris & Paula Bailey and Family Tanrallt Road. Gwespyr.

Chapter 1

An Introduction

I have been asked to write a small history book about the Scala Cinema as a building from when it first was opened.

First I must acknowledge all the people who have helped me to collate this information. First Friends of the Scala, Mrs Sandra Pitt, Chair and Mr Frank Bailey Vice Chair. The Records Office at Hawarden, Record office at Ruthin run by Archivist Mr Mathias who was most helpful and the North Wales Press Owners of the Prestatyn Weekly for the copyright, giving permission to publish and also Harry Thomas who has supplied some of the pictures. The Birkenhead records office, Cllr Dugan at Bangor who gave me names of Saronie owned Picture Houses in North Wales, and of course many anonymous donors who have been willing to give me their time and stories for this book. Thanks to all these many varied people. Thanks to Sophia Drew M.B.E. for helping me put my words onto a computer and Frank and Lilian for proof reading the final copy.

Before I start on the theatre, I must describe the ancient village which became the town of Prestatyn which is on the North Wales Coast between the Dee Estuary and the River Clwyd at the East of the future tourist destination of Rhyl, between the mouth of the River Dee and the River Clwyd. The history of the town goes back to Stone Age times and the artefacts that have been found prove that the Round House found close to the Roman Bath House at the bottom of Melyd Avenue during excavations, was built during the Bronze Age. When the Romans arrived here about 73AD and stayed till 225AD and left Britain or Albion as the Romans called it, in 410AD.

The Saxons arrived as the Romans left and ruled for 600 years and called this area Englefield (Old Flintshire) which went up to the River Clwyd. This area was shared with the Vikings after Alfred the Great`s agreement.

Offa built his dyke in 8th Century between 779 and 797AD from Chepstow to Prestatyn and was it built to form a boundary between Mercia and Wales for taxing purposes possibly.

1066 came with the Normans and they called this area Atis Cross.

In 1164 Henry II gave us the a stronghold called Prestatyn Castle and it was occupied by Ricardo Banistre and in 1167 the town and the stronghold were destroyed by Owain Gwynedd and Banistre moved to Lancashire.

We did have a Linen Industry in Prestatyn but that was ruined when Owain Glyndwr came along and destroyed the town in 1401. There is a map showing the flax fields and the Duck Pond along Gronant Road which was not only driving the wheel to grind the corn it was also the retting pond where the flax was immersed for three weeks before it was dried and separated into threads to be woven into linen material.

The tide used to come to the bottom of Glyn Avenue and the Woolworths area in the eighteenth century and was called Cwr-y-Traeth (surround of the beach).

The High Street was formed by a stream running down Ffordd Las, forming a gully. Evidence is by the inclines one has to climb to get out of High Street, Maes y Groes, Fern Avenue, Top Car Park, Priory Lane, Church Walks and Christ Church is built on a bank. It is said to be the steepest High Street in Britain. People lived by the stream for water.

In 1794 the Cut was made and to protect the cut, the sandbank was made which went parallel to Grosvenor Road which is still there today although much reduced in height. King George III's government did this to create more land to grow crops due to losing trade with the continent because of the long wars in the Continent. The Francs and French were trying to starve Britain into submission and the English King had to grow food for his subjects.

Mr Pochin between 1880 and 1882 came to Prestatyn and built another sandhill as we see it today because he wanted to build a beach house on the land he had salvaged by keeping the sea out with this high sand dune. Cwr y traeth became a marsh fed by hillside streams. This is the land that the Scala which was built as the Town Hall in 1900, was built on. When the modern builders tried to drain the land at what is now Ffordd Parc Bodnant Housing Estate, it lowered the water table in Prestatyn in the lower part of the town and buildings subsided including the Scala . It had to be closed to the public in December 2000 for health and safety reasons.

In 1898 a gent came to Prestatyn to set up a business as a solicitor with an eye to doing many conveyances for the houses needed for the growing town. His name was Ffoulks-Roberts and he built the semi-detached houses, three stories high in Nant Hall Road and today they are now made into flats. Ffoulks-Roberts lived in the farthest one from the town called Ashlands and he brought his children from Denbigh because of the drains being poor and there was Diphtheria. The children went to Miss Hickson's High School in Marine Road next door to Horeb Chapel.

Above and overleaf - Mr and Mrs Ffoulkes - Roberts with their family at Nant Hall Hotel.

L to R overleaf Arthur Dad Ella Peter Mother with David

Photograph courtesy Ruthin Records Office

They then went to Pendre School, Ffordd Las in 1904. Mr Ffoulks-Roberts telephone number was `Prestatyn 1` in the new national telephone company`s directory. He said there was no culture in Prestatyn after he had lived here for a while and set about doing something about correcting the deficiency. He found the site and the builder a Mr Thomas Jones who had a flair for design so things got underway to build four shops with an entrance to a theatre in the centre of the shops. It was ready for July 1900.

Arrangements were made for a Grand Opening. It was a remarkable speculation when you consider that in the 1901 census there were 1261 souls in Prestatyn including children to build a theatre in the town. The design was a credit to the neighbourhood. The facing bricks were Ruabon pressed bricks with strings of Gwespyr stone and Dennis terracotta steps. The main entrance was a collapsible sliding gate that moved horizontally, folding doors opening outward. The entrance hall had a stair case to the gallery and the audience had a clear passage to the street. The pay box was adjacent to the staircase. Two vestibule doors lead to the main hall. The hall was sixty feet by forty eight feet. I was brought up on £.S.D and so the modern measurements were 18m x 14m.

The hall was said to hold 800 to 1000 standing. I imagine the Black Hole of Calcutta. Ugh!

Illumination was by Gas Lamps, the gas from Mr Pochins Gas Works which he had built for himself and the town. Heating was by high pressure water pipes by Kings of Liverpool. The stage protruded into the hall with steps each side. With doors on the stage leading to anti-rooms with fire grates and access to toilets.

The kitchen and boiler house were at the rear of the stage and four distinct means of exit in times of emergencies. Acoustics were very good due to the height of the ceiling. The stage lighting was by limelight which is a lit gas jet played onto a piece of burnt limestone. It created a very bright light. Sometimes spot lamps would be used, a lamp fitted with an acetylene lamp. This could be very dangerous without due care and caused a lot of fires in theatres throughout Britain.

Furnishings were supplied by Williams and Richards of the Emporium at the top of Prestatyn High Street. The name is still there today. They could supply floor covering, linoleum, carpets, curtains, furniture, clothing of all sorts, anything from swaddling clothes to a shroud and a funeral to go with it.

Before the buses came that took people to Rhyl, Prestatyn was the shopping centre for Gronant, Llanasa, New Market (Trelawnyd) and Dyserth and Meliden. People walked to town during this time.

The opening of the town hall was Thursday 26th July 1900 at 1.30pm. Some of the shops were not finished and not for fifteen months. The hall was set out for lunch, three tables laid out on the carpeted floor. The flag was raised and stuck half mast. Someone suggested the pole should be sawn off above the flag so it looked full mast. A ladder was found and the rope untangled so the flag was fully raised to the top. Bunting was strewn all over the building giving it a festive appearance.

The building was forty feet (12 metres) high. Prestatyn people were on a fete day all dressed up in their best and gathered in front of the town hall. A large company assembled in front at 1.30pm when Mr and Mrs Ffoulks-Roberts arrived with the children. Applause. Then Mr John Jones, Chairman of the Council, of `Sefton`, Nant Hall Road, (was Park House is now Park Surgery,) was a partner in the brickworks in Ffordd Isa and supplied the bricks for the town hall.

At 1.35pm the arrival of Mrs L E McLaren with her son caused more applause.

Mr Ffoulks-Roberts stepped forward to greet her and her son, followed by Mr John Jones who greeted them, then asked her to open the Town Hall. They moved towards the entrance. Charles McLaren could not be there because as an MP he had other functions to attend and sent his apologies.

Master Ffoulks-Roberts presented Mrs McLaren with a bouquet of flowers when a bee settled on them and there was an immediate kerfuffle, the bee flew off and things returned to normal. Miss Ffoulks-Roberts presented Mrs McLaren with the key of Silver Gilt on a cushion of blue plush.

The key was supplied by Mr H Stanfield, Jeweller of Prestatyn. It was in a Silver Gilt Case with Mrs L E McLaren written on one side and Prestatyn Town Hall on the other. Also presented to Henry McLaren was a picture illuminated by Hudson and Keens and presented by Mr Edwards, Welsh representative of the firm. It had a picture of the recipient and a medallion of Golden Grove, Llanasa. It was framed and a work of art. Mr Pochin had changed the name of Gull Grove to Golden Grove.

After the presentation, Mrs McLaren kissed the two children, put the key in the lock and said, `I declare this building open.` Then thanked those present for the welcome. The party was photographed. They entered the hall where there were three handsomely laid out tables with flowers, etc and Mr Jones officiated. Lunch was served in a first class manner by Mrs Thomas, wife of Mr Thomas, Manager of the Nant Hall Hotel. There were seventy five invited guests.

The menu consisted of the following dishes:-

Fish Salmon Mayonnaise.

Joints included Roast Beef with
Horseradish Sauce,

Roast Lamb with Mint Sauce,

Roasted Chicken, Glazed Tongues,
Pressed Beef.

Green Peas and Young Potatoes.

Oyster Paté.

Followed by:-

Trifles, Empress Tart, Eclairs,

Parisienne Pastry,

Strawberries with Ice, Cheese and Salads.

Coffee

*(There was no mention of drinks but the following speeches were
powered by alcohol)*

Opening of the Town Hall, Prestatyn. 26 July 1900.
From the Rhyl Journal

After the Banquet speeches at Town Hall.

The Chairman said several letters of apology had been received from gentlemen who had intended being present. Dr Griffith wrote expressing the opinion that Mr Ffoulks-Roberts had stimulated trade in the district.

The Toast of the Queen having been received with honours, the chairman proposed the health of Mrs MacLaren. That was the first time he had had the honour of meeting that lady in public and that was the first occasion that she had taken part in a public function in Prestatyn (hear, hear). As Chairman of the Council he had pleasure in welcoming the lady to the town (applause). He hoped that it was the first of many public gatherings she would be present at (applause). He thought that Mrs MacLaren was not rightly understood by the people of Prestatyn. Until a short time ago he was one of those who did not understand her, and had thought that there was a gulf between her and the people of Prestatyn. But latterly he had found that the differences between them were really very small, if they existed at all (applause). The more they understood one another and the more they come together the better it would be for the prosperity of Prestatyn. Mr and Mrs MacLaren's position with regard to a growing place like Prestatyn was a difficult one. It was difficult to understand what direction the developments would take. Prestatyn was bound to go ahead, and that the nearer they came together and the better they understood each other, the better they would be able to work together for the prosperity of Prestatyn, and naturally for Mr and Mrs MacLaren (applause).

The toast was received with much applause, and on rising to respond Mrs MacLaren was received with cheers. After thanking the company for the way they had received the toast, she said she was afraid that she did not deserve half what had been said concerning her. In coming that day to Prestatyn it had afforded her great pleasure to perform the small ceremony of opening the doors of that building.

She congratulated them upon the acquisition of such a beautiful hall (applause). For the success of Prestatyn there were three elements necessary. The first element was Mr John Jones - (applause) - the second was Mr Goronwy Jones, and the third Mr A Ffoulks-Roberts (applause). By the combined efforts of those gentlemen they had a boldness of plan, an artisticness of design, and a power to carry it out which could not be equalled by any other three citizens (applause). In what respect their policy and their special traits and character excelled was a mystery they could not fathom. At all events she advised them to follow the lead of those three gentlemen, in everything they did for the future of Prestatyn (applause). That was the course she intended to adopt and pursue: she was therefore justified in recommending it to them (applause). They must not, however, forget what the other inhabitants of Prestatyn had done. She remembered well the first time she saw Prestatyn, and she was not very pleased with it (laughter). Prestatyn at that time consisted of a solitary street with thatched cottages on each side of it. It suffered from two great terrors: the flooding of it by the water from the sea and the dearth of water from the hills (applause). They had combated more or less those difficulties, and she must say that since then the property owners had risen to the occasion in a manner that had surprised her. There was hardly one owner of property in the High street who had not spent a considerable sum of money to cope with the growing demands of the place (applause). When she first came to Prestatyn she had to bring with her a truckful of luggage; now all she required was a trunk, as she found that she could procure in the town all the necessaries, and many of the luxuries of life (applause). Things were as cheap and good as in many towns of much greater size (applause).

When observing what their tradesmen had done they must not forget what the public bodies had done. They had provided churches and chapels for the spiritual accommodation and needs, as well as schools for the educational requirements of the town (applause). They had also elected and secured the services of a very eminent body of men of their District Council (applause). She must say that she felt very much indebted to these gentlemen for their labours in the public service. They were all busy men whose time was money, and they gave a good many hours' anxious thought to the affairs of Prestatyn (applause). She thought that the people should be very grateful to them. The great problem that day before the District Council themselves was how to go ahead without being too far ahead (applause). Of course they could not have a fire engine before they had a fire (laughter and applause). Nor could they have a Town Hall before they had a town to put it in (applause). Thanks to Mr John Jones, Mr Goronwy Jones, and Mr A Ffoulks-Roberts they had a Town Hall (applause). People told them that they should wait for a demand before they provided the supply. But that was a principle of the tradespeople who lived in the days of Alfred the Great (laughter). Our modern tradesmen took a different course: they created the demand by first providing the supply (applause). She hoped shortly to see buildings erected on the shore, which would give Prestatyn people a sea front of eligible houses. She knew that some said that there was no demand for such houses, but it was quite plain that if those houses were put up, lodging-house keepers would take them, and visitors would come and occupy the rooms (applause).

Providence had blessed her with a son, and she trusted that when his college career was over he would be able with his youthful energy to solve some of the problems connected with the development of Prestatyn (loud applause). There was one point she would like to touch upon before sitting down and that was their host Mr Ffoulks-Roberts (applause). She understood it was due to him that they owed the possession of that hall for Prestatyn (applause). They much rejoiced that Mr Ffoulks-Roberts had seen his way to cast in his lot with Prestatyn people, and had invested his capital there, giving them the benefit of his intelligence as to what Prestatyn required (applause). She thought in designing that hall he had shown a very wonderful forecast of what Prestatyn required, and had met it. Mr Ffoulks-Roberts had not only built that hall for material purposes, but he had considered it his duty to try and raise the intellectual tone of Prestatyn (applause). He had provided a place where the flowers of rhetoric could grow, and the twin arts of music and the drama could find an abiding home (applause). He was also entitled to their deepest gratitude and all the support they could give him. She hoped that the opening of that hall would mark a new era in the history of Prestatyn (loud applause).

The public were here admitted to the gallery of the hall.

Mr H D MacLaren next proposed "Prosperity to the Hall and Town of Prestatyn," and said that the opening of that building marked the development of Prestatyn from a village to a town (applause). It was necessary that every town should have its hall, where music could be encouraged and enjoyed, and where both sides of public questions could be debated. Zeal was necessary for the welfare of a place like Prestatyn (applause).

Mr J B Linnell responded to the toast, and said he was sure that as Prestatyn became better known it would rapidly develop. It was the place that Liverpool people were delighted to visit, and he advised the investing of capital in the town (applause).

The Chairman also responded, and said that he had looked with pleasure at the progress of Prestatyn, which had developed from an insignificant village to the dignity of a seaside health resort (applause). He concluded by giving the toast of the visitors.

Colonel Lloyd Williams, Major Webber, and Mr R Llew Jones (Rhyl) responded.

The Chairman then presented Mr H D MacLaren with an address, which had been subscribed to by the members of the District Council. In making the presentation, Mr Jones said he was sure that Mr MacLaren would cherish the address, and that he would realise his own responsibilities, as he could do a great deal of good or he could do harm. In everything he should look to the Almighty for guidance (applause).

Mr John Pritchard, Mr J E L Jones, and Mr Thomas Williams also spoke, and congratulated Mrs MacLaren and her son of the excellent addresses delivered.

The proceedings closed with the drinking of the health of Mr John Jones.The toast of Mr Ffoulks -Roberts was omitted at his special request.

During the luncheon Mr Wm Jones (Denbigh) gave sections on the harp.

Quote from Chair of Prestatyn Urban District Council, Councillor John Jones, ` I am pleased to welcome Mrs McLaren here today who is now closer to the people of the town.`

In answer Mrs McLaren replied,`All three gentlemen involved in the design of this building must be congratulated for the future of the town for this building which is magnificent. You can`t have a fire brigade without a fire, just as you can`t have a Town Hall without a town which these three men have achieved. Prestatyn suffers from two main problems, one was water from the sea and the other was a dearth of water which was now controlled by Pochin`s pipes.`

Mrs McLaren was a bit of a Charlie Dimmock of her day and was seen laying paving stones and curb edges as if she was one of the workmen at Bastion Road which her father Mr Pochin was building as part of the development of the town as access to the beaches on the land he had claimed where his own beach house was built.

She also did a lot of physical work at Bodnant Gardens to make it as it is today. The first house the Pochins had at Llandudno had remarkable gardens at Haulfre. I believe the gardens are open to the public today.

On the day of the Town Hall`s opening, she provided a tea party for all the children of the town at the National School which is on the corner of Bastion Road and Marine Road and today is an Indian Restaurant.

26th July 1900 in the evening of the opening day, a Grand Concert was held at the Town Hall given by the Prestatyn Choral Society renowned throughout North Wales, conducted by G W Jones, Head Master of the British School. Mendelssohn's `Come Let us Sing` and Schubert's `Song of Miriam.` were two items and there were soloist singers and instrumentalists which entertained the audience. Intermezzo soloist sang `Forget me not` as a sample of the one of the songs. In the interval Mr J Jones, Chair PUDC, asked Lady Mostyn of Talacre to address the audience on the claims of the Nursing Institute which she did in a few well chosen words. Mr Rev. Jewel responded on behalf of the British and National School as they were beneficiaries of the proceeds of the concert. And just to mention, the Pochin Family were Quakers.

Mr Pochin gave the town water and gas and lifted Prestatyn out of the Middle Ages to a modern town during the 1880`s.

Chapter 2

The Introduction of Culture to Prestatyn

The Town Hall had a variety of shows, a mixture of entertainers, local and some from away. The Eisteddfod which was sponsored by the Welsh Congregationalists had been held in Prestatyn prior to the Town Hall being built. They were held in the Bardic Circle above the Panoramic Shelter area. (Mr King had the shelter built in 1928 by Whitley Brothers.) The stones are not laid out in the Bardic style with the positive entrance to the East. The Eisteddfod ran till 1914 at the Town Hall after it was opened and did not re-commence after the end of World War 1 in 1918 due to lack of enthusiasm.

Some of the early stars at the Town Hall were Jimmy Charters Senior, a great Liverpool comedian, a touch of the Ken Dodds so I was told. Mrs Pochin nee Agnes Heap from Warrington, read poems in the Lancashire Dialect and unfortunately died in 1904.

The building was not complete for 15 months, i.e. the shop and the clock tower above. The builder had put some newspapers of the time in a niche and plastered it over. When Mr Saronie was having the Town Hall refurbished years later, these items were found like a time capsule in a similar manner that has been done during the rebuild of the New Scala by Prestatyn Town Council. The papers found were the Rhyl Recorder and Advertiser, today the Rhyl Journal, the news of 25th October 1901 from Colwyn Bay Welsh Coast Pioneer and programmes of the previous fifteen months of the shows at the Town Hall.

The Gilcrist Lectures were held as talks on a series of subjects. One talk was on Spiders and Dr Andrews` subject was on Brains and Nerves. It was sixpence a lecture or five shillings for the series with reserved seats. On other nights Hot Pots were given by Mr Littler, Grocer, and Mr Lloyd, Baker, with entertainment. The Town Hall was in use for all sorts of functions, religious services, sacred concerts, etc. Mr Ffoulks-Roberts must have been pleased with his enterprise.

In 1903, General George White came to talk about the relief of Mafeking after the Boer War when the Boers submitted to British rule 1902.

A new time capsule filled by school children, town council and friends of the Scala was installed in the new Scala on 23rd April 2009.

Prestatyn Town Hall 1903...before the
South and North Wales Bank was built.
Today it is the HSBC bank.

Chapter 3

The Coming of the Picture House.

Thomas Edison who had a workshop of skilled people who invented things and patented them, forgot to register one invention in Europe. William Dickson who worked for Edison made an early picture show called Kinema Show, which was a continuous film, forty feet long, a sort of 'What the Butler saw'. So the Luminaire brothers in France put their films in reels, made a hand turned projector with a bright light and gave a show in the basement of a Paris Hotel with the use of a screen. They had invented the cinema. But first they had to invent a mobile animated camera , in order not to infringe Edison's patent.

On 5th November 1909 we had our first animated picture by a group lead by Miss Regna Lehn. They stayed for ten weeks in the Town Hall. The Pictures `The Wild Goose Chase` caused screams of laughter and `Save my Dog` another comedy.

The problem Miss Lehn had was that she only had one projector so while the reels were being changed live entertainment was offered. She sang `Days beyond recall` the song of the time. The dancing was in flowing dresses with scarves. The idea was to get the ladies out of those iron sprung corsets with seventeen inch waists. The type of dancing was couples and individuals, Isadora Duncan style. Isadora was riding in an early car and the scarf which she always wore caught in the rear wheel and she was strangled.

Mr Holland Roberts, a secretary to Mr Ffoulks-Roberts and Manager of the Town Hall, tried to show films for a while. Then the Bearing brothers came to show films on 23th September 1911. In the advertisements only the best films were shown and the rest were rubbish. It was mostly from July to Christmas that they opened the hall for films.

The opposition was in the Victoria Hall. It was in the Mews of the Victoria Hotel and showed films and live shows including pantomimes. They had tea and biscuits at the interval which the Town Hall did not.

During 1898 Jim Roberts showed films at Ty Caradoc, the British School. He played a gramophone invented by Emile Berlina who had emigrated to America. The records were made from pressed glass or aluminium. There were animated pictures down Sandy Lane run by travellers of the gypsy types.

Projectors were about sixty pounds. Some made their own films.

On 25th November 1911 there were two plays performed in Welsh.

On 6th April 1912 the Prestatyn Dramatic Society presented `David Copperfield`.

On 17th August 1912 the Boult Bee Cadets took over the Town Hall and they played Matinees. Very Talented Entertainers.

On 12th July 1913 in the Prestatyn Weekly, a supplement of Saronie`s Enterprises was included in the paper. **He had arrived!**

J R Saronie as he called himself, installed a new electric generator, powered by gas supplied by PUDC Gasworks, which had been purchased in 1910 from Mrs McLaren by the council. So his theatre was all electric except for the kettle ring. Programmes started at 7pm till 10pm and you could come and go as you wished. There were usually four different films. Also lots of serials. It was like Eastenders, Coronation Street and Emmerdale Farm. Pictures changed Mondays, Wednesdays and Fridays and sometimes Thursdays, Fridays and Saturdays. Local dramatic societies played in the hall when pictures were not showing. Please remember all the films were silent with subtitles and the Town Hall was always full in the summer.

Miss Grindon was Saronie`s pianist. She was connected with Vale View School on Meliden Road.

Chapter 4.

Saronie and the Cinema.

Saronie was a photographer in Liverpool. It was quite a lucrative business taking pictures before people left these shores for the far flung regions of the Empire. They were not Governors or Ambassadors. They were skilled workmen going to the different parts to teach people in those countries to be tradesmen. One called Ossie Jones, Prestatyn, went to Lagos in Nigeria to teach woodwork, as an example. Saronie was asked to take photographs of Edward VII when he stayed at Ruthin Castle. The King used to go there for the shoots and other attentions or attractions. He was 'amorously involved' with Lady Cornwallis, who used to wave him goodbye at Ruthin Station as she shouted `Bye, bye, Teddy.`

Mrs Saronie was asked to take pictures of Harry Lauder who appeared at the Argyle Theatre in Birkenhead. Before television, the radio or BBC always had a show on Saturday night at peak times from the Argyle. It was one of the highlights of the week and was broadcast nationally.

Back at the Scala and Saronie at great expense showed 'Antony and Cleopatra'. Must be seen. Saronie did not advertise for a couple of weeks to save money perhaps. Saronie refurbished the Roller Skating Rink at Birkenhead and turned it into a luxurious picture house in the middle of the Great War. I don`t think he could have done that during WW2.

It was called the Electric Palace.

Boxing reports were popular news items shown by Saronie as part of the news films that he introduced to the people of the area. Bombardier Wells v. Sergeant Dixon were country champions at the time. He showed the Territorial Army at the Front in Belgium. The original regulations for the `Terriers` were for the defence of the Homeland but the army was so short of soldiers, the regulations were changed in 1915. Throughout the war, Saronie showed films taken at the front whenever they were available.

From a photographer to a cinema owner, Saronie must have been a shrewd business man. He had two cinemas in Birkenhead, two cinemas in Bangor, one in Kinmel Camp during the Great War and the Scala in Prestatyn. And there may have been others.

The Coliseum Cinema, Old
Chester Road, Birkenhead

SARONIE'S

PICTURE .

PALACE,

Old Chester Rd., Tranmere.

Under the direction (locally) of
M. SARONIE.

PROGRAMME of the

World-Famed

Royal Biograph,

Latest and Best

Animated Pictures

Ever Produced.

Educative, Instructive, Sensational and Topical.

ENTIRE CHANGE OF PROGRAMME WEEKLY.

First Best in 1896 and still unsurpassable.

EVERY EVENING AT 8.

MATINEE SATURDAY AFTERNOON AT 3.

On 20th May 1914 at the Town Hall, the Pendre School pupils demonstrated dancing the Tango and the Brasilue, new steps to Prestatyn.

Where Saronie Court Flats are at the Top of the High Street, Saronie bought that piece of ground and developed the Arcadian Gardens. He supplied an Alfresco Theatre, illuminated the gardens with electric lights and the opening night was Saturday 30th May 1914 and presented the people of Prestatyn with entertainment by `The Tip Tops` a company from London.

The entertainment competition for the Town Hall were for the Ariston Pierrots back at their old usual places in July 1914, the Beach and the Penisadre Orchard where Boots Chemist is today. Tension was mounting in Europe with the threat of war. Germany had asked the King of Belgium if the German Army could pass through Belgium to attack France because the German Secret Service said the French had plans to strike at Germany through Belgium and King Albert said `No!!!!!!`. So the Germans attacked and shelled Liege, in North East Belgium on 4th August 1914.

Britain declared war on Germany at midnight on 4th August 1914.

We had fears in Prestatyn of air strikes from German Airships and there was a blackout. Due to the blackout, although Mr Saronie allowed the Pierrots to complete their show on 5th August 1914, entertainment finished throughout Prestatyn at night except at the Town Hall. And it was then that the Pierrots left Town.

There were 130 airship raids on Britain, most on London during the Great War. The Belgium Army fought the Germans for two weeks, lead by King Albert and gave the British and French time to mobilise. The Belgium refugees went to Holland in their thousands and some came to Britain. It must have been a minor Dunkirk. Those that came to Prestatyn were sorted in the Town Hall and Mr Ffoulks-Roberts gave one of his houses in Nant Hall Road, called the `Lilacs` for six months. Kelston Farm, Llanasa, `Durlston`, Gronant Road, Prestatyn and other small houses took in refugees. E.g.. Number 3 and 7 Purbreck Terrace and the Gem Cottage. Meetings were also held in Bethel Chapel Hall, High Street.

The Roman Catholic Priest was Pierre de Pere who came with the Belgians.

There was a letter sent by Mr Ffoulks-Roberts to the Prestatyn Weekly dated 11th October 1914. It read:-

Sir

As there seems to be some misunderstanding on the point, will you allow me some space in your paper, to say that all applications for the hire of the Town Hall should be made in the first instance to Mr Leonard Hughes, Solicitor, Prestatyn who has now the management of the Town Hall on my behalf. Thank you

Yours

A.Ffoulks-Roberts.

This meant that Saronie was only a tenant of the Town Hall.

Dated 14th October 1914 there was a letter in the paper thanking Mr Ffoulks-Roberts for the use of the hall but there is no mention of who sent in this letter.

SARONIE'S ELECTRIC PICTURES
TOWN HALL, PRESTATYN

SPECIAL ATTRACTION FOR THREE NIGHTS ONLY.

Monday, Tuesday and Wednesday

THE GREAT KHAKI BOXING CONTESTS for two Championships.

BOMBARDIER WELLS v. SERGT. DICK SMITH.
CPL. PAT O'KEEFE v. L.-CPL. JIM SULLIVAN.

Thursday, Friday, and Saturday— OFFICIAL WAR OFFICE FILM—

MACHINE-GUN SCHOOL AT THE FRONT.

And full Programme of exclusive features.

Doors open 7-15, commence 7-30. Saturdays—Doors open 7; Commence 7-30.
PRICES AS USUAL. Special Terms for Soldiers and Sailors.

SARONIE'S ELECTRIC PICTURES
TOWN HALL, PRESTATYN

CHANGE OF PROGRAMME THREE TIMES WEEKLY
Every Monday, Wednesday, and Friday.

Monday and Tuesday, **THE BLUE FLAME.**
Drama in two Parts.

Wednesday and Thursday, **PAWNS OF FATE.**
Sensational Drama.

Thursday, Friday, and Saturday— OFFICIAL WAR OFFICE FILM—

WITH THE INDIAN TROOPS AT THE FRONT (No. 2.)
Exclusive Pictures from the Firing Line. On no account miss this Series.

Doors open 7-15, commence 7-30. Saturdays—Doors open 7; Commence 7-30.
PRICES AS USUAL. Special Terms for Soldiers and Sailors.

SARONIE'S Electric Pictures
TOWN HALL, PRESTATYN.

LOOK OUT FOR THE BATTLE OF THE SOMME
October 5th, 6th, and 7th.

Monday, Tuesday Wednesday—Sensational Film : 3-part Drama
THE MILLIONAIRE BABY.
Thursday, Friday, and Saturday - Three-part Drama.
THE ROAD OF MANY TURNINGS
Commencement of the New Serial: "TERENCE O'ROURKE."
Dont' miss the opening episodes.

Prices of Admission (No. Tax) Body of Hall 7d.

SARONIE'S Latest Enterprise.

Arcadian Gardens, High Street, P

Proprietor and Manager: M. SARONIE   Resident Manager: LLEW. WYNNE.   Stage Manager: SANDY WHIT

GRAND OPENING OF THE SEASON: SATURDAY EVENING, MAY 30th, 1914.

M. SARONIE presents   "THE TIP-TOPS,"   A Company of SPECIALLY SELECTED ENTER

UNIQUE MUSICAL MELANGE IN GORGEOUS DRESSES AND STAGE SETTING.

GARDENS BRILLIANTLY ILLUMINATED WITH ELECTR

WHIT MONDAY.—SPECIAL MATINEE at 3 o'clock.—Full Dress Performance.

GRAND ALFRESCO ENTERTAINMENT

EVERY AFTERNOC
COMMENCIN

ADMISSION:— SEATS, 6d. and 3d.; PROMENADE, 2d.   CHILDREN, 3d. and 2d.

Nov 11 10th, 1917.   PRESTATYN WEEK

SARONIE'S Electric Pictures

TOWN HALL, PRESTATYN.
MARCH 15th, 16th, and 17th.
MATINEES DAILY

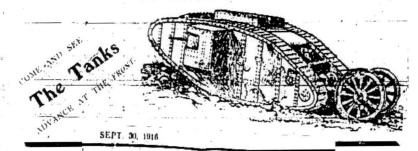

COME AND SEE The Tanks ADVANCE AT THE FRONT.

SEPT. 30, 1916

SARONIE'S Electric Pictures

TOWN HALL, PRESTATYN.
CONTINUOUS PERFORMANCE: 6 to 10 p.m.

Thursday, Friday, and Saturday, October 5th, 6th, and 7th.
MATINEE EACH DAY AT 3.

BATTLE
OF THE
SOMME

"See that this Picture which is in itself an epic of self-sacrifice and gallantry, reaches everyone. Herald the deeds of our brave men to the ends of the earth."—Lloyd George.

SARONIE'S ENTERPRISES.

LA SCALA, Prestatyn

ALL WEEK, commencing Monday, April 19th :

"TOMMY ATKINS IN BERLIN,"

THE GREATEST SUPER COMEDY OF THE YEAR.

PHENOMENAL ATTRACTION EVERYWHERE SHOWN.

In Addition to the above :—

MONDAY AND TUESDAY—
　"SELFISH YATES," featuring Wm. S. Hart.
　"ELMO THE MIGHTY" Episode 13. *Gazette.*

WEDNESDAY AND THURSDAY—
　"LOVE SUBLIME" featuring Wilfred Lucas & Carmel Myers
　"THE GREAT SECRET" Episode 11. *Topical Budget.*

FRIDAY AND SATURDAY—
　"THE SIREN'S SONG," featuring Theda Bara.
　"HIS LYING HEART," Comedy.

MATINEE SATURDAY, 2-30. Children Half-price.

On 15th January 1915 Saronie showed films of the Front as a regular feature as they became available. 20th February 1915 there were lots of soldiers in the district. Some were under canvas, others billeted in houses around the area.

On 29th March 1915 a military concert was held at the town hall with admission free. A soldier was on a shilling a day (5p per day) but it was all found and clothing. The Chairman was Colonel Gwyn, Commander of the Ambulance Core, part of the RAMC. Local characters took part and Nellie Davies, Contralto, was one of Carol Vordeman's relations. Thomas Jones, Tenor, Frank Nichols, Baritone, who was killed by a horse some years later as he crossed a field where a full blood stallion was and Frank's singing disturbed it and it attacked him. He had been warned.Charlie Chaplin was making a regular appearance with dozens of short films.

15th April 1915 - a film showing the Prince of Wales visiting the first line of trenches when he visited the guards. He would have become King Edward VIII but for his 'attachment' to the divorced american Mrs Wallis Simpson.

10th May 1916 "The Four Feathers" was the film. It has been re-made countless times since.

17th May 1916 a film on how Britain prepared for the war was shown, eighteen months too late. And "She" by Rieder Haggart.

17th June 1916 Lord Kitchener visits the trenches. He was the man on posters who was always pointing at you "Your Country Needs You." He was in charge in the Boer War and did unmentionable things in Concentration Camp.

10th March 1917 "Come and see the tanks, a British Invention".

17th April 1917, Mr Saronie bought the Town Hall from Ffoulks Roberts. And the Ffoulks-Roberts family, now grown up, said `Dad was well pleased with the bargain.` I should like to know what the price was?

On the 14th September 1918 the sign over the Town Hall was taken down.

On 7th December 1918 the lights of Prestatyn were all on after the war.

3rd April 1920, the new name `La Scala` was put up. In Prestatyn Weekly, 15th April 1920, Mr Saronie had been asked to accept the candidature for a seat on the Birkenhead Town Council recently rendered vacant through the death of Mr John Harrison. Mr Saronie, as is well known, had much experience having served for a number of years on the Tramways, Sanitary and Road Commissioners of Birkenhead council.

A great extension of the boundaries under the control of this body is shortly to take place. A new residence for Mr Saronie on the Prestatyn Hillside is now near completion under the hands of Mr W D Prescott and will shortly be ready for occupation.On 12th June 1920 the Palladium was proposed by the Prestatyn Palladium Ltd for a capital of £28,000 and built by Roberts and Sloss of Lancashire, wealthy builders of the time. The site was the orchard of Penisydre Farm where Boots Chemist is today. The Palladium was to have an upstairs café with dance hall. The new theatre was to seat 900 to 1000 people, three shops and a bank. The bank was Williams Deacons, now the Royal Bank of Scotland. There must have been some prior financial arrangements. The Palladium was built and shops were ready before the cinema was ready. The Bank arrived in 1925. This was in competition to Saronie Enterprises. It had its own generator for electricity.

County-Borough of **Birkenhead.**

The Mayor (Mr. David Roger Rowlands)

requests the pleasure of the Company of

Mr Councillor and Mrs. Saronie

on the occasion of the Presentation of the Honorary
Freedom of the Borough to
The Right. Hon. Lord Birkenhead,
the Lord High Chancellor of England,
in the Assembly Room, at the Town Hall, Birkenhead,
on Monday, the 28th day of April, 1919.
Ceremony at 3 p.m.

The favour of an immediate reply on the accompanying form is requested,
as admission will be by Ticket only.

TOWN HALL,
BIRKENHEAD.

TEA WILL BE PROVIDED.

LOWER FRONT ENTRANCE

SARONIE   FOR GRANGE.

LADIES AND GENTLEMEN.

At the invitation of the Conservative Party, I have consented to become a Candidate for the vacant seat in Grange Ward ; and I beg to solicit the favour of your suffrages.

I am a native of Merseyside, and have lived in Birkenhead practically all my life. I have watched its steady development into a great and thriving industrial community with satisfaction and pride, and if you honour me with your confidence it would be my earnest desire to take a part in directing its future destinies.

This is a most important period in the history of the Borough. Large schemes of development are under consideration, some of them fraught with great possibilities ; and, if carried out, involving considerable expenditure. These will have to be very carefully watched, especially from a Birkenhead point of view, and I venture to think that my business experience would be of service to the ratepayers in dealing with these questions.

I am a large ratepayer in the town. For sixteen years I carried on business in Grange Road, and I fully realise its importance as a commercial centre. To the trading community economical administration of our public affairs is a matter of the utmost concern ; and, as a business man, you may rely with complete confidence upon my endeavour to keep the rates at the lowest possible level.

I am a firm supporter of denominational teaching in our schools ; and, as one who has always been in close touch with the working classes, every movement calculated to raise the standard of industrial life in our town would command my sincerest sympathy.

Yours faithfully,

JAMES SARONIE.

25, CAVENDISH DRIVE,

12th July 1920 – Tommy Atkins in `Berlin`. Three main pictures per week.

13th August 1920 – a silent version of `Firefly` was shown at La Scala accompanied by piano music played by Mr Stagg. The romance of Tarzan in nine episodes was also shown during this period. No Johnny Weissmuller.

2nd August 1920 Saronie had the Town Hall in Rhyl. `Auction of the Souls.` Adults only. Seen by 50,000 people in the Albert Hall, London and also a comedy called `A Box of Vestas`

13th August 1920 – a concert at the Arcadia Gardens entertained alfresco style by the Sun Spots from the Hippodrome, London.

This was all part of Saronie Enterprises. Every week the Sun Spots changed their name during the holiday period. 15th August 1920 at the Arcadian Gardens a Grand Opera Concert including Welsh Prima Donna Soprano L Evan Williams, Miss Myrtle Jones, Contralto and Eva Lewis, famous Welsh Tenor.

OCTOBER 9th, 1920.

La Scala Super PICTURE HOUSE, PRESTATYN.

DOUBLE FEATURE PROGRAMME:

Monday and Tuesday, October 11th & 12th : Dorothy Dalton in **Other Men's Wives.**

Marguerite Clark in **Girls.**

Weds. and Thursday, October 13th & 14th : William Desmond in **Closin' In.**

"A Woman in Grey." Episode 3.

Friday & Saturday, October 15th & 16 : Alma Reubens in **The Restless Souls.**

All Week : Charlie Chaplin.

October 29th New Serial, "BARRABAS." First Episode.

Saturday—Matinee 2-45 ; Continuous 6-30 :

Monday to Friday—7-30 Nightly.

15th May 1921 the Palladium was opened with a big concert.

During 1921 there were no advertisements at the cinema or Arcadia Gardens due to Influenza Epidemics following World War 1.

In 1922 February 25th the Prestatyn Urban District Council issued a warning about the `flu epidemic which spread around the world killing millions. More people died than during the war.

Use a handkerchief wherever possible, stay away from crowds, keep warm. The popular phrase at the time was `The Spanish lady has arrived.` This was reported in the Prestatyn Weekly. This because Spain was not in WW1 but it reported epidemics freely but countries in the war kept quiet. `Flu seemed to attack late teens to middle age people. The young and the elderly seemed to be immune. The remedy: Brine or Salt Water or Borasic, frequently swill the nose with the mixture, gargle with a spoonful of salt dissolved in warm water, laced with permanganate of potash.

17th August 1923 Saronie takes over the Palladium, Saronie Enterprises. (Saronie by this time hired out La Scala for live theatre entertainment by Prestatyn Dramatic Society, lectures and other functions such as politicians giving talks on theory and principles. I didn`t know they had any.)

Expensive entertainment at the Palladium when Saronie took over was by the band of the Coldstream Guards by kind permission of Colonel Steld, Commanding Officer, CB, DSO, CMG. The Director of Music Lieutenant R G Evans, LRAM.

SARONIE'S ENTERPRISES.

Sole Proprietor: M. SARONIE.

Arcadian Gardens, Prestatyn
SUNDAY, AUGUST 15th.

Grand Operatic and Instrumental
CONCERT

ARTISTES.
Madame L. EVANS-WILLIAMS
(The Welsh Prima Donna).

Miss MYRTLE JONES
(Contralto). London and Provincial Concerts.

Mr. EVAN LEWIS
The Famous Welsh Tenor.

Mr. DAVID BRAZELL
The Celebrated Baritone.

Mr. PURCELL JONES
The Eminent Cellist.

Mr. IDRIS LEWIS
(at the Piano). London and Provincial Concerts.

Doors Open 7-30, Commence at 7-45.
Prices 3/6, 2/4, 1/3 (limited). Book Seats at once.

ARCADIAN GARDENS.
WEEK COMMENCING AUGUST 15
Every Evening at 8. Doors open 7-30.

THE IRRESISTABLE
7
Sun Spots
From the London Hippodrome and Victoria Palace.

MATINEES WET AFTERNOONS at 8.
Box Office Open, 10 to 12, 8 to 5.
RESERVED SEATS 1/10; UNRESERVED 1/3 and 9d.

LA SCALA
Super Cinema.

Double Feature Programme, For 2 Days Only
FRIDAY AND SATURDAY, AUGUST 13th & 14th.
TOM MIX IN
THE WILDERNESS TRAIL

WM. D. GRIFFITH'S
MASTER FILM PRODUCTION
"BROKEN BLOSSOMS."

Twice Nightly, 6 and 8-15.
Book Your Seats at Once.

NEXT WEEK.
Another Stupendous Programme

August 16th and 17th
The Bond of Fear
Featuring Belle Bennett.

August 18th and 19th
The Chinese Puzzle
Featuring Leon M. Lion.

August 20th and 21st
City of Dim Faces
Featuring Sessue Hayakawa.

Continuous Performances, 6-30 till 10.
USUAL PRICES.

Printed and Published by J. T. Burrows, Prestatyn, in the County of Flint.

SARONIE'S ENTERPRISES.

Sole Proprietor: M. SARONIE.

ARCADIAN GARDENS

WEEK COMMENCING AUGUST 30,

Every Evening at 8.   Doors open 7-30.

FRED ARNOLD'S

"Box o' Vestas"

under the personal direction of
ARTHUR FORBES.

ARTHUR FORBES, Comedian.

ALLAN WILLIAMS, Tenor.

FRED PAYNE, Light Comedian and Dancer.

CONNIE BISHOP, Contralto and Monologue Artist.

BILLIE BELL, Soubrette and Dance.

MARGARET STEPHENS, Soprano.

VICTOR RAYMOND, At the Piano.

MATINEES WET AFTERNOONS at 3.

Box Office Open, 10 to 12, 3 to 5.

RESERVED SEATS 1/10;
UNRESERVED 1/3 and 9d.

LA SCALA Super Cinema

NEXT WEEK.

Another Stupendous Programme

August 30th and 31st:

The Maternal Spark,

Featuring Irene Hunt

September 1st and 2nd:

GENERAL POST

BRITISH SUPER PRODUCTION
Featuring Lilian Braithwaite

September 3rd and 4th:

Green Eyes,

Featuring Dorothy Dalton

All Week: **Charlie Chaplin** in "Carmen" (4 reel).

Come and see yourself in the Carnival Procession! Showing one week only.

Continuous Performances, 6-30 till 10.

USUAL PRICES.

Printed and Published by J. T. Burrows, Prestatyn, in the County of Flint.

40

ARONIE'S ENTERPRISES.

LA SCALA, PRESTATYN.

THREE DAYS ONLY.   COMMENCING THURSDAY, JULY 1st, 2nd, 3rd.

"Auction of Souls"

EXACTLY AS SHOWN AT THE ROYAL ALBERT HALL, LONDON.

 Featuring **AURORA MARDIGANIAN.**

SYMPHONY ORCHESTRA AND CHORUS.

Once Nightly at 7-30 prompt.   Matinees Thursday and Saturday at 3.

RESERVED SEATS (BOOKED) 2/4; 1/3 (Limited Number).   ADULTS ONLY.

SARONIE'S ENTERPRISES,

Sole Proprietor: M. SARONIE.

ARCADIAN GARDENS

WEEK COMMENCING AUGUST 23.

Every Evening at 8.   Doors open 7-30.

ONE OF THE FINEST PARTIES TOURING

Percy H. Holmshaw presents the famous

ROYAL,
Vaudervillians

in an entirely new production.

MISS MAY ROYAL,
The Brilliant Entertainer from the Palace, London.

MISS BOBS GLADWYN, Flautist.   Soprano.

MISS MARJORIE WYNNE,
Violiniste.   Contralto.

MISS MADELINE GLADWYN, At the Piano.

J. RUPERT FAIRBANKS, Tenor.

ROB E. DOUGLAS, Comedian.

SANDY FRASER, Scotch Humourist and Dancer.

THE GLADWYN TRIO, Musical Ensemble.
Piano, Voice, Flute, Piccolo, Violin, etc. From the
Principal London and Provincial Theatres.

MATINEES WET AFTERNOONS at 3.
Box Office, Open, 10 to 12, 3 to 5.
RESERVED SEATS 1/10;
UNRESERVED 1/3 and 9d.

LA SCALA Super Cinema

NEXT WEEK.
Another Stupendous Programme

August 23rd and 24th :
SPECIAL SUPER PRODUCTION:
Henry Waltham in
THE MAN WHO FOUND HIMSEL

August 25th and 26th :
Captain of His Soul
Featuring William Desmon
Lightning Bryce. Episode 11.

August 27th and 28th :
Romance of Lady Hamilto
Featuring Malvina Longfellov

All Week : Charlie Chaplin in "The Millio
Dollar." Usual Comedies and Travels.

Continuous Performances, 6-30 till 10.
USUAL PRICES.

LA SCALA,
SUNDAY, AUGUST 22nd, 1920
The Celebrated CYNTHIA
MALE VOICE QUARTETTE
And Full Concert Party, under the
Direction of

MR. BEN BAKER

Commence 8 prompt; Doors open 7-30.
PRICE 1/3 ONLY.

Printed and Published by J. T. Burrows,
Prestatyn, in the County of Fli

PRESTATYN PALLADIUM LTD.

2 - 6 - 1920

The prospectus of a new company—Prestatyn Palladium Ltd.—has just been issued. The capital is £28,000.

The prospectus states—

The Company has been formed for the purpose of acquiring freehold land in High Street, Prestatyn, with the object of erecting on the site an up-to-date and attractive Picture Hall, shops bank premises and cafe.

The site is an ideal one, situate as it is in the centre of the shopping district, close to the Railway Station, and opposite the Town Hall Buildings. The town is a favourite seaside resort, and is rapidly growing. It is the first watering place along the Welsh Coast after leaving Chester. Plans have been prepared for the erection of a substantial, attractive, and economical building to accommodate 920 persons. The plans, which include three shops and bank premises in front, with an up-to-date cafe over the shops and bank, have been approved by the District Council and the licensing Authority. The shops, bank premises, and cafe will be let to tenants and will bring in a substantial revenue. The Directors have already received numerous applications for these premises.

Among the names of Directors is that of Mr. James P. Linnell, Surveyor, Prestatyn,

SARONIE'S ENTERPRISES

Sole Proprietor: M. SARONIE.

FOR WEEK COMMENCING JULY 19TH, 1920.

ARCADIAN

Assistant Manager: W. L. FRASER.

Every Evening at 8,

ALBERT LYON'S

Summits

High Class Concert Party.

Prices : 1/10, 1/3, and 9d.

1/10 Seats Booked in Advance.
Box Office Open, 10 to 12, 3 to 5.

MATINEES WET AFTERNOONS at 3.

LA SCALA
Super Cinema.

JULY 19th : **THE VAMP,**

Featuring Enid Bennett.

JULY 21st : **WHO WILL MARRY ME ?**

Featuring Carmel Myers.

JULY 23rd : **CHASING A FORTUNE,**

Featuring George Walsh.

Prices : 1/3 and 9d.

MATINEES WET AFTERNOONS.

Printed and Published by J. T. Burrows, Prestatyn, in the County of Flint.

Chapter 5

La Scala is very well used.

1920

12th June the Palladium was proposed. A £28,000 company was formed, plans offered to Prestatyn Urban District Council and were approved.

The site was the orchard of Penisadre Farm where Boots Chemist is today. The Palladium was to have an upstairs café with a dance hall. The new theatre was to seat between 900 and 100 people, three shops and a bank. The bank was Williams Deacon, now the Royal Bank of Scotland. So there must have been some prior financial arrangements.

The Palladium was built and shops were ready and let before the cinema was ready. The Bank arrived in 1925. This was in competition to Saronie Enterprises.

It had its own generator for electricity and was built by Roberts and Sloss.

(see page 43)

13th August a silent version of `Firefly` was shown at La Scala accompanied by piano music played by Mr Stag. `*The Romance of Tarzan*` in nine episodes was also shown during this period. (no Johnny Weissmuller).

12th July `Tommy Atkins in Berlin` and three pictures per week.

2nd August Saronie had the Town Hall in Rhyl, `Auction of the Soul`, adults only, seen by fifty thousand people in the Albert Hall, London, and also a comedy called `A Box of Vestas`.

13th August a Concert at the Arcadia Gardens entertained alfresco style by the `Sun Spots` from the Hippodrome, London. This was all part of Saronies Enterprises. Every week the Sun Spots changed their name during the holiday season.

15th August - the Grand Opera at the Arcadia Gardens on a Sunday. Welsh Prima Dona Soprano L Evan Williams, Miss Myrtle Jones, Contralto, Evan Lewis, famous Welsh Tenor.

1921

There were no advertisements for either the cinema or the Arcadia Gardens during this year due to the influenza epidemic that followed World War 1.

1922

In July Flintshire Eisteddfod was held in Prestatyn. In the Prestatyn Weekly there is a picture of the occasion held on the Hillside at the Bardic Stone Circle.

A concert was held on behalf of Doctor Barnardo`s on 12th December at the Arcadia Gardens.

Throughout 1922 and 1923, trenches were dug in Prestatyn High Street to lay sewer pipes. There was trouble with water particularly at High Tides. The road surface under the tarmac was cobble stones, some boulder clay, then sand and pebbles, then peat at eight feet deep. That was what they wanted to lay the pipes in. This was the time when the `Prestatyn Lady` skeleton was found directly in front of the Scala and opposite Penisadre in the peat layer. Gilbert Smith, Architect and Surveyor, was sent for since he was an amateur archaeologist. He referred it to a Professor from the Royal College of Surgeons, Professor Sir Arthur Keith who identified the bones from 2,500 BC of the Neolithic Period. They were removed to the Royal College of Surgeons, London which was sadly bombed during WW2. They are now believed to be in the National History Museum. The High Street was in turmoil. By this time Saronie was fed up with obstructions to his customers going to his theatre.

No further advertisements of functions at the Scala during 1922.

Home entertainment with gramophone seemed to be popular getting a few friends together who did not have flu.

27th April, the Palladium was opened with a Concert. `The Martyrs`, a dramatic cantata. Wilford Roberts, Baritone, a local High Street Butcher whose shop still exists today opposite the Parish Church and run by his own Grandson, in the High Street, took part.

1923

After Saronie moved to the Palladium, La Scala fell back into plays, concerts, lectures and charity shows and such. The Arcadian Gardens were hardly used and became an eyesore. Mr Rowlands, a shoe repairer called a cobbler in those days, took over the entrance and pay box to do repairs for his customers at the gardens. He was there for many years.

La Scala Super PICTURE HOUSE, PRESTATYN.

Monday and Tuesday, October 25th & 26th:

Special Double Programme:
Charles Ray in
Hayfoot Strawfoot.

Bryant Washburn in
The Poor Boob.

Weds. and Thursday, October 27th & 28th:

Jack Richards in
By Proxy.

"A Woman in Grey." Episode 5.

Friday & Saturday, October 29th & 30th:

Dorothy Gish in
Turning the Tables.

MARVELS OF THE UNIVERSE.

A New Exciting Serial, **Barrabas.** Episode 2.

Charlie all Week.

MARY PICKFORD in her latest "**HEART O' THE HILLS**"
Showing November 4th, 5th, and 6th.   Now booking.

Saturday—Matinee 2-45; Continuous 6-30.
Monday to Friday—7-30 Nightly.

48

Mrs Saronie

Mr Saronie

Saronie stood for election for PUDC. He did not get elected. If he had used his proper name, Jim Roberts, he would have been elected. People don`t like phoney names.

10th and 11th May at La Scala, the Prestatyn Dramatic Society put on the play `Elijah Comes to Stay` in aid of the Motor Ambulance Fund.

Later in 1923, 13th and 14th November, Prestatyn Dramatic Society staged at La Scala `Barbara` by Jerome K Jerome, famous author of `Three Men in a Boat`.

13th December at La Scala, Musical Entertainment. Mair Jones, Soprano of Queens Hall, London and other artistes in aid of the Motor Ambulance Fund. The town lacked an ambulance which it needed as it grew. Some time in the past an inebriated lady who had been to a public house in Gwaenysgor, fell down one of the Hillside quarries and was killed. So the policeman at the accident site took the door off a nearby house, gathered four men and they carried the body down to the police station. After this episode, funding was found for a stretcher ambulance. It had a cover over the injured so they could take the patient by train to Rhyl or Chester hospital. The stretcher was kept at the police station at 1, Nant Hall Road, Prestatyn. Eventually enough funds were raised to buy a second hand motor ambulance. It was an ex-army van on a Daimler chassis. It was a sleeve valve engine. Then later a Ford V-eight small lorry chassis and the old body transferred so it looked very smart painted cream. Finding support for funding was very poorly sponsored. Vincent Smith, Secretary of the Ambulance Association of The County Garage on Meliden Road. (Long gone.) was in charge of fund raising.

There was a tale that Miss Smith daughter of Vincent Smith, married to Mr Jones, used to send down his ham and mustard sandwiches with one of the boys from the county garage who would eat the ham and present Mr Jones with the hamless sandwiches and on this strength of neglect, the straw that broke this particular camel`s back, he divorced her through this unwitting omission.

During the early 1930`s Mr Vincent Smith paid for a driver and provided accommodation for the ambulance. Mr Smith with council connections, knew that the council could claim financial support for the ambulance with ARP funds as World War Two approached. So, frustrated by lack of financial backing, he drove the vehicle to the council yard and handed it over, lock stock and barrel. I don`t know why they had an attitude at the council.

The ambulance had a good suspension, not like modern ones where you feel every bump. That was 70 years ago.

Friday August 17th 1923, Saronie Enterprises take over the Palladium. He had expensive entertainment with the Band of the Coldstream Guards by kind permission of Colonel H W Studds, CB, CMG, DSO and he commanded the Coldstream Guards. Director of Music, R G Evans, LRAM.

1924.

23rd February, a Welsh Play at La Scala `Tu Hwnt yr Lien`, the Chair was taken by Dr Tudor Griffiths.

13th February a Grand Concert on behalf of the Fire Brigade was held a La Scala.

The Fire Brigades in towns and villages were run as charities but not in the larger cities. When WW2 broke out, all the fire brigades were taken over by the Government and after the war, by local authorities. The Fire Engine and the building were owned by the Local Authorities, paid out of rates but the pre-war staff were voluntary.

27th March, a Grand Concert at La Scala on behalf of Dr Barnardo`s Homes, Chaired by the Vicar.

20th October at the Palladium, Saronie`s Enterprises showed `The Hunchback of Notre Dame.`

There were two or three pictures per week, not of great importance but fifty two weeklies per annum and two or three pictures per week makes it one hundred and four pictures per year was a lot of main feature films so I have picked out the best. Star Status came with the `Talkies` with the exception of Charlie Chaplin, Mary Pickford, Buster Keaton, Rudolph Valentino, Pearl White, Ronald Coleman, Laurel and Hardy, Fatty Arbuckle, Paul Muni, Loretta Young, Marie Dressler and many others.

1925

18th January `Sodom and Gomorrah` was shown in the Palladium.

5th January at La Scala a Grand Musical with three harpists.

18th February at the Palladium, Mary Pickford in `Dorothy Vernon of Haddon Hall.

26th February , La Scala, a concert on behalf of Prestatyn Fire Brigade.

10th March, La Scala, Grand Benefit Concert on behalf of Mr P Gould Roberts MP Conservative. Mr Wilford Roberts, Baritone, took part in many concerts at La Scala and the Palladium.

9th April, The Palladium, `The Ten Commandments` augmented by a full orchestra for the full effects.

13th May, Prestatyn Weekly reports that a Ffoulks-Roberts, Solicitor, of Denbigh and Prestatyn, three charges of fraudulently converted to his own use, monies entrusted to him for investment, adjudged himself bankrupt. He was 60 years of age. He was admitted as a Solicitor in 1887. The last time his books were audited, 1911, he showed a loss of £38,011. Gross liabilities £96,537.00 in 1925. To rank for a dividend, £52,280.00 with his assets of £14,266.00. The case to be continued later. Mr Ffoulks-Roberts applied for bail and supplied three sureties of £500 each. On 20th June 1925, at the Ruthin Assizes, unsecured creditors 84, 58 of these claimed an aggregate of £51,355.00. He pleaded guilty to five cases. The judge said the country was shocked. He was sentenced to five years penal servitude. The Judge said it would have been more but for his age of 61 years. These figures are as printed.

It makes you wonder?

He carried out his sentence in Parkhurst, Isle of Wight.

Whilst Saronie had the Palladium, he brought stage shows to La Scala during the visitor season. Such as:- Super Severn Concert Parties, Delight that appeared at the Royal Command Performance at Marlborough House, Fancy Fair from Crystal Palace, The Royal Arcadians, The Zeal Players, Pro Rata, Royal Quixotes, Speed.

This was repeated every summer. The many groups that entertained included:- The Music Makers, The Makeup Box, Keep Moving, Frills and Flounces and the Mascots.

1926

The Gilcrist Lectures took place at La Scala. It was founded in Lancashire to educate the willing to learn in 1888.

13th January the Rev. Cranage, subject `How the Monks Lived in the Middle Ages.`

24th January, `The Marvel of the Tiny – the study of electrons.`

20th April, `Early Man.` by Gilbert Smith from the recent results of local researches.

Many more lectures of this calibre were given.

1927.

3rd and 4th March, La Scala, Prestatyn Dramatic Society presented `Lilies of the Field.`

2nd April La Scala, Mia Hall Dramatic Society presented `A Little Bit of Fluff.`

25th May another Welsh production by Talagoch Society, `Y Ffon Dafl.`

6th June the summer shows were back for the season. Same names, same people.

No outstanding films this year.

29th June there was a Solar Eclipse.

Electricity comes to Prestatyn. The first commercial premises to be fitted out with it was the little shop in Kings Avenue, now a hair dressers.

23rd December, a Sacred Concert at La Scala.

1928.

29th and 30th April, the Prestatyn Dramatic Society presented at La Scala `Aren`t we All.` in aid of the Motor Ambulance.

20th October Frank Nicholas, renowned singer, was killed. He performed at La Scala often and was killed accidentally by a stallion when Frank crossed his field and the horse did not like his voice, so my father told me later.

23rd December a Sacred Concert on behalf of the Prestatyn Football Club. Wilford Roberts sang at this concert.

During the life of La Scala, there were three billiard tables in the Green Room run by the Liberal Association.

1929.

(The year of the Wall Street Crash.)

6th July Gramophone record entertainment at La Scala. Artists of the World. You could buy a record you liked.

Wireless Sets were becoming popular. 120 volt High Tension Battery, 9 volt grid bias battery, a 2 volt accumulator which was a glass or celluloid case with two lead plates within filled with sulphuric acid could be recharged for 6d (2.4 p) or 9d (4 p) at the local wireless shop or local garage. Then came an attachment you could plug in to the household electricity supply which did away with batteries. It was called an Eliminator. To be followed by the mains sets which were a complete unit.

24th September, `Country Life`, a Pastoral Story presented by a local group and lasted four days.

11th October at La Scala the Prestatyn Dramatic Society presented `A Tight Corner.`

24th October, Black Thursday. The collapse of Wall Street in America.

As a result of this world wide financial catastrophe, many local builders in Prestatyn went bankrupt due to not being able to sell the properties they had built since no-one could get mortgages. Something that is happening today in 2008.

27th December, a Grand Concert in aid of Prestatyn Football Club at La Scala.

The Hillside Gardens were under development during the `30`s. Mr Taylor who had a market garden where the High School is now, gave hundred's of plants from his market garden free. The local unemployed worked up there for a few hours per week and they had a voucher for 10/- groceries. The depression hit Prestatyn hard until Courtaulds built their factory at Greenfields.

Saronie supplied goldfish for the pond in Hillside Gardens but cats and the light fingered helped themselves. But that is life.

When Saronie bought the Town Hall, the deal included the shops and eventually one of his tenants was Mr George Brookes. He sold tobacco and had a barbers shop. Mr Brookes employed a barber and ran an illegal betting shop. He always had a couple of bookies runners, one operated from the Cross Foxes down the street and the other from the Victoria Hotel to George Brookes` shop. You could place a bet on the phone or by post. So you paid for your bets after the event. The police could raid an illegal betting shop without a warrant. That was the law. So on Derby Days and Grand Nationals, George was often raided. Anyone in the shop would be loaded into the Black Maria, before the JP and fined £50. In 1960 it became legal to have a betting shop so George said to Saronie that he wanted to open a betting shop. Saronie objected. Mr Radcliffe took over and opened his sweet shop. Mr Radcliffe gave some of these details.

1930.
A New Name for La Scala to the Scala.

8th March, the talkies came to the Scala. Saronie left the Palladium and went back to the Scala. The Theatre was refurbished, the roof was raised, new seats, stage altered and new entrance with sales area and speakers mounted and Neon Lights were put on the front of the building.

20th March the first talkies with Maurice Chevalier was in `Innocents in Paris` at the Scala.

The Palladium converted to sound a few days later by the gentleman who took over the lease again this time from Saronie who had gone back the The Scala.

When Mr Saronie brought the talkies to the Scala, his pianist, Mr Stag, lost his job so he became a Postman. Mr Stag lived in Maes y Groes with his family, the home he had acquired since living in Prestatyn. He was from Merseyside.

The first recognised talkie was `The Jazz Singer` with Al Jolson. It was sound on records and now and again either the sound or the record would get out of sync.

The first words spoken in a movie were `Wait a minute, wait a minute. You ain`t heard nothing` yet.` That was Al Jolson played on three discs.

The full history on Google is worth reading.

22nd November 1930 a story of a German soldier in WWI `All Quiet on the Western Front` and it was emotional. It made the point that people are much the same everywhere. It is the stupid leaders with their egos. They are not left handed or right handed but underhanded. Will it ever change?

1931.

14th March - information Prestatyn Weekly. A short article about Joseph Griffin, a resident of Prestatyn, who sang with the d`Oyley Carte Opera Company who were appearing at the Royal Court Theatre, Liverpool. Mr Griffin toured with the company. He was a brother to Mrs Wilford Roberts, High Street, Prestatyn. Mr Griffin sang in `Princess Ida`, `HMS Pinafore` , `Ruddigore`, `Pirates of Penzance`, `Trial by Jury`. Just thought I would mention this in passing.

24th August. Charlie Chaplin in `City Lights.`

Most of the films by this time were talkies. Many of the silent film actors became redundant because their voices were not suitable for the sound track. Rudolf Valentino, a great romantic, using his posture and eyebrows to create atmosphere and the beautiful ladies with scratchy voices were out of a job.

Laurel and Hardy moved from `Silents` to `Talkies` with great success and they made forty eight films to my knowledge.

1932.

With the arrival of the Talkies came the Star Status for the actors/actresses.

1st June – Greta Garbo and Raymond Navarro in `Mata Hari` a spy of WWI.

27th July - `Frankenstein`, the doctor who made a human being that turned out to be a monster. Not suitable for children and no children allowed in. Boris Karlof, the monster, that the kids loved to dress up as.

23rd August, `The End of the Rainbow` with Richard Tauber, the world`s best tenor at the time it was said.

27th August – Sir Alan Cobham `Air Circus` at Aberkinsey Farm. 15 aircraft, one autogiro invented by a Spaniard, two airliners, 'Hermes' by Handley Page, and onto the site, 1/3d with cars 1/-. All sorts of stunts, people standing on wings whilst the aircraft flew. The Rhyl councillors had a free flight but landed in tree. Nobody was hurt. What a laugh. The wings were so big they could land at 30mph.

19th November - `The Desert Song`, the Red Shadow played by John Boles, romance and deception

1933.

The Death of Lady Aberconway, Mrs McLaren, died at the Chateau de la Garoupe in the South of France. She was brought to Bodnant Hall, Aberconwy and interned in the family mausoleum. She was the lady who opened the Town Hall in 1900. Lady Aberconway had made gardening her life`s hobby with much artistic skill and taste. The beauty of Bodnant Gardens was due to her. The Chateau de la

Garoupe is also a place with a beautiful garden of which she was the ruling spirit. She once said that you must love your 'gardener and never let a grumpy savage near your treasured pleasuances'.Lady Aberconway was a charming hostess keenly interested in politics especially questions affecting women since her mother, Agnes Heap, had been a suffragette. And it was she who complained why did women have to pay a penny at public conveniences for what men did for nothing. Lady Aberconway was a Dame of Grace of St John's of Jerusalem and a CBE for her work during WWI. She was a mother of two sons and two daughters. Her second son was killed in action of the Royal Flying Corps in WWI.

4th February – Gracie Fields in `Looking on the Bright Side`. Gracie was in many films once talkies had arrived. She didn`t act, she played herself. But from cotton mills to a British leading Film Star and the millions she made. Her voice was exceptional and the film was on at the Scala for a whole week with a `house` full every night.

17th April `Sally Bishop` with our local writer and actor Emlyn Williams of Ffynnongroew and Holywell Grammar School.

Sunday Cinemas when there was always an argument particularly with the clergy because they were afraid of losing their congregation. I remember Rev Iestin Jenkins saying from the pulpit, I quote, `There are more stories of human frailty and aggression in the bible than Hollywood ever thought of or even dare to screen. If only people would look and read it.` But he was different and could overfill the Presbyterian Church every Sunday evening. He was a show on his own.

When the war broke out quite a number of chapel boys were called up with the Territorials and we went to church that evening on 4th September 1939 and he said, `If you think of a sin that you are about to take part in, think of this pulpit.` He was in the trenches in WWI.

14th August, at the Scala, `King Kong`. A story by English novelist Edgar Wallace who spent time in Africa and wrote 174 novels. `King Kong` was a remarkable film of clever technicians but I did not find it scary, not like `The Mummy` with Boris Karlof. I went to see this film with my Dad who had just finished putting tiles over the bathroom sink. The archaeologist in the film standing next to the upright sarcophagus removed the lid and the body came to life after over 4000 years and the bandages started to fall away as he walked out of the sarcophagus. He had been bandaged alive for some misdemeanour. And on our return home, Dad found all his tiles had fallen down into the sink. A double shock to us.

28th August - `the popular musical `Forty Second Street` and still being produced on stages all over the world.

There was a new full length film often twice a week and in the same week 200 years before, the Bishop of St Asaph married a 14 year old beautiful young lady. She had a fortune of £20,000. At that time women could marry at the age of 12.

I just thought I would mention it. Pious and procuring somebody always lets the side down. Human frailty.

1934.

John Jones from `Sefton`, Nant Hall Road, died. He was the opening chairman when the Town Hall was opened by Mrs McLaren in 1900.

Mickey Mouse makes an appearance in films at the Scala in `Steam Boat Willie`. Tune into Google for Mickey Mouse History. Interesting. Walt Disney was established and his products don`t date.

January. Woolworths open in Prestatyn. 40 galvanised buckets for the first 40 customers.

Saronie liked boxing and showed Max Baer v. Canera fight. Max Baer won. He was later in two or three films and was a natural actor.

8th October. Gracie Fields in `Sing as you Go`.

1935.

Robert Donat in `The Count of Monte Christo`.

And lots of Laurel and Hardy films, via Harold Roache Productions.

Fred Astaire and Ginger Rogers in `The Gay Divorcee`.

Mae West `Going to Town`.

Classics like `Jane Ayre`.

3rd January Saronie held a party for 1,250 children, a New Year Party with Alderman Richard Thomas of Bangor. He did the same at the Scala for the Prestatyn children.

30th December the first Technicolour Picture was advertised and was shown in 1936.

1936

Beccy Sharp, all colour. Surpasses anything you have seen on the screen based on the story of `Vanity Fair`.

6th January `The Crusaders` film with Loretta Young and Herbert Wilcoson.

20th January 1936. King George V died.

27th January `The Glass Key` with George Raft.

1st February and Saronie showed the Funeral Procession of George V.

It was in both Technicolour and Monochrome.

13th February, W C Fields in `The Memory Expert`.

6th April, Fred Astaire and Ginger Rogers in `Top Hat.`

17th September, Bing Crosby in `Anything Goes.`

1937

9th January - `The Trail of the Lonesome Pine` - the first all outside colour picture. Sylvia Sidney and Fred McMurrey.

8th March – George Formby in `Keep your Seats Please`.

15th March – Paul Robeson and Alan Jones, bass and tenor in ` Showboat`.

27th March – Laurel and Hardy in `Our Relations`. And Will Hay in `Windbag the Sailor`.

15th April – Katherine Hepburn and Frederick March in 'Mary of Scotland`.

14th June – William Powell and Myrna Loy in ` The Great Ziegfeld`.

12th May – Coronation of George V1th.

18th May – Shirley Temple in `Dimples`.

24th May – Coronation in Technicolour and Monochrome of the full service in the Abbey.

30th August – Saronie was interested in boxing and had the film that kept us up all night - `Joe Louis v. Tommie Farr` at the Yankee Stadium, New York. Joe was put down in an early round but after fourteen rounds won on points. Joe Louis thought Tommie Farr had won till the points were counted. Tommie Far was said to have been the seventh best fighter from Wales for all time. Vincent Smith, the Boss, took all the staff to the Scala to see the fight on film. All Fourteen Rounds.

23rd September 1937 – there were no Air Services to USA in those days. I stayed up all night to listen to the fight on our new Echo Radio that cost 14 guineas. People all over the world listened to the fight because Joe Louis was considered the best of the day. Tommy Farr had a pub in Brighton by the station during the war. I got slung out because I sang ` Sosban fach a berwy ar y tan.` He had not got a singing licence. Tommy Farr had a good grip on my collar. I went back the next day and apologised and had a free pint. He was a gentleman.

1938

3 – D Colour Film. Sometime through the year we had 3-D pictures. We were given cardboard glasses as we went into the Scala. One lens was blue and the other was red. When you looked at the film through the glasses it was scary to see a train running over you. People on swings almost hitting you in the face with their shoes. Also riding on a sledge was a good effect. Stampedes of horses and cows rushing at you. Thousands of films were made all over the world and shown at pictures houses and on Television and for me `Casablanca` 1942 in Black and White with Humphrey Bogart and Ingrid Bergman is about the best out of all the thousands I saw. Bogart was likely the finest male actor ever and Hepburn was the likely finest female actor ever seen on the screen. (`African Queen` with Bogart and Hepburn, the prim and proper lady and the rough sailor, what a wonderful pair.)

A phrase you don`t hear any more – I bought it on the Never, Never.

Film Stars had become a feature of the film world. Gary Cooper and Spencer

Tracey brought in more film goers if they were in the film such the one they both starred in - ` Sky Devil`. Also Bill Boyd as Hopalong Cassidy made numerous cowboy films and the fact that he was in it meant thousands would flock in to the picture houses to see Hopalong rather than Bill Boyd. He was too clean to be a cowboy anyway. Barbara Stanwick who became very rich and her ranch was half the size of Wales.

14th February – Prestatyn needs a public hall for all sorts of functions as we had when we had a Town Hall – said a letter by Annie Williams, 12 Victoria Avenue.

12th March – George Formby with his Ukalele `Keep Fit`.

26th March – Fred Astaire and Gingers in `Shall we Dance`.

9th April – Anna Neagle and Antony Walbrook in `Victoria the Great.`

30th March – Gary Cooper and George Raft in `Souls at Sea`.

30th April – Eleanor Evans JP became the first lady vice Chair to Vincent Smith Chairman of Prestatyn Urban District Council.

14th May – Tyrone Power and no mention of the female star was in `Lovely to Look At`.

5th May – George Sanders and Peter Lorre in `Lancer Spy.`

26th May – Shirley Temple in `Hide`.

25th May – Paul Newman in `Scarface`. A true Gangster film.

   Zane Gray Westerns were very popular at this time.

21st May - `Dinner at the Ritz` with Paul Newman.

28th May – Kathleen Hepburn in `Quality Street`.

4th June – Eddie Cantor in `Ali Baba Goes to Town`

7th July – Dorothy Lamour and John Hal in `Hurricane`. How he tied her to a tree and of course himself to save them being swept away.

29th July – Emlyn Williams in `Dead Men Tell No Tales`. Emlyn was from Ffynnongroew and became a famous playwright and actor who was very often to portray very violent characters.

13th August – Councillor Vincent Smith saw an advert in a newspaper that a company was looking for a site in the North West of England to build a Holiday Camp. This was because Billy Butlin was moving people out of London by the thousands every weekend in the summer to holiday camps in Skegness and Clacton-on-Sea by LNER out of Kings Cross. The LMS wanted a piece of the action so they joined up with Thomas Cook and searched for a site in North West England. Cllr Vincent Smith answered the advert saying a large acreage was available in Prestatyn and being on the council, he had available the information. This lead him to going to London to meet the new company Thomas Cook and LMS (London, Midland and Scottish Railway Company) headed by Lord Stamp, Chairman of LMS. A company was set up with £250,000 for a self catering camp with 1,100 chalets, fifty eight acres using £140,000. Surveyors and architects arrived at Prestatyn and they got things under way. It was an awful winter. I was driving a site vehicle at the age of 16. It was hard work with a hand wound tipper. The camp had to be ready for Spring 1939. It was said that it was all British material but the walls of the chalets were made of sawdust shavings covered with plaster on site. The walls came from Germany, the materials Hitler used for his youth holiday camps `Strength through Joy`.

18th August - David Lloyd, famous Tenor and local boy from Ffynnongroew at the Pavilion, Rhyl with the Halle Orchestra.

20th August - `Rebecca of Sunny Brook Farm with Shirley Temple who was a wondrous child who became an ambassador for the USA as an adult.

7th November – Sonja Henie in `Happy Landings`, she was a famous ice skater from Scandinavia but no actress.

By kind permission of Mr J R Saronie, the WVS opened their Headquarters in the Scala Green Room. The WVS started in Plymouth Town by Sheila Isaacs, Lady Dowager Marchioness of Reading on 1st January 1938. Lady volunteers of usually middle class ladies initially formed to support the ARP. The WVS gathered momentum with a pamphlet `What can we do?`.

Films of the Spanish Civil War brought the troubled atmosphere of war and Gurnica raids on newsreels and which later was painted by Picasso and brought the message home.

During bombing, the safest place was the corner of the room if you were without a shelter. The Germans bombed Plymouth April 1941. Five raids reduced the town to rubble. Initially the WVS did not have a uniform, just Cap Badges but later hats and overcoats by Digby Morton and they had to be purchased by the ladies. The WVS philosophy was ` If a job wants doing, it was done.` The WVS organised evacuees at both ends of their transport with labels on everybody including mums and children. 1.5 million people were moved when war was declared, canteens set up in caravans in some places. At the time of Dunkirk, spits were set up to cook meat for the returning troupes along the South coast.

1939

14th January – Pat Collins, the amusement entrepreneur who had sites in South Wales and Colwyn Bay wanted a site in Prestatyn. The Pendre Site was available. It was owned by Mr Saronie and Mr King, the man who built the Panoramic Shelter in 1928. It was put before the council. Cllr Eleanor Evans said `I don`t want an amusement site at the bottom of my avenue. Put it in Kings Avenue` and Cllr Plimmer who lived in Victoria Avenue said `I don`t want it in my backyard either` and Cllr Corbet – Ellis said, `Put it on the old circus site `. (where the market is today.)

The Prestatyn Estates did not want it there either. Pat Collins had offered to build a Public Hall at Pendre. The area was bigger then than the memorial gardens are today.

So the council settled with Pat Collins for the site where the bus station is today. So it was Roundabouts and various entertainments though the argument went on for 4 weeks in the Prestatyn Weekly.

You must remember the Foreshore was not owned by PUDC at this time but by Prestatyn Estates, i.e. The Aberconway Family. They wanted all their land to be let on lease and for this area they wanted 1/- (5p) per square foot for a Ten Year Lease.

23rd January – Gracie Fields in `We are Going to be Rich`.

War was coming according to Councillor Alderman Geo Williams and he arranged for a Calcium Carbide Factory at Llanerch y Mor, something for the manufacture of armaments. There was a £16,000 Hotel to be built at the Ffrith with 40 bedrooms but due the war, this was abandoned.

27th February – Lesley Howard – in `Pygmalion` by George Bernard Shaw which later made into a musical `My Fair Lady`.

4th March – advertisements for the chalets at the holiday village by the sea. Rates per week all found. Between 24th June and 8th July £3 per person. From July 8th to September 9th £3.10s per week per person. And from September onwards, £3.

8th April – Errol Flynn and Olivier de Haviland in `The Adventures of Robin Hood`.

Mrs Groom dies after an accident with a bus. Her funeral was attended by many Romanies and Pat Collins paid for the funeral. I don`t know what happened to her classic gypsy type caravan, whether it was burnt according to Romany Lore, or if it was removed from Pendre site. Mrs Groom was brought up in South Wales. A marriage to a Norwegian was arranged by her mother, but she would not sleep with him. She slept in a tent in his garden of his house. Eventually they divorced and she went to live in Hamburg, Germany and entertained English sailors in a type of club. She returned to London and was in a stage show as a dancer. She was a beautiful woman and was painted about thirty times by Dante, Gabriel and Rossetti. Immortalised on canvass, once on the parapet of Notre Dame Cathedral, Paris. She came to live in Prestatyn about 1914. Her second husband Mr Groom was a writer of novels, Gypsy Folk Lore, Gypsy Tents and Scottish Border History. Mrs Groom kept hens and her caravan was immaculate. She was a striking lady even in old age.

22nd April – respirators were distributed in Prestatyn in little cardboard boxes about 7" cube. They had a piece of string to carry over your shoulder.

Eleanor Evans, became First Woman Chairman of PUDC.

Plans for evacuees from Wirral and Birkenhead in particular of 1200 children.

24th June – Lord Stamp declares the Thomas Cook LMS Holiday Camp (Tower Beach) open and a banquet was held. All the titled people from miles around were invited, probably share holders in the Railway Company. Also Councillors from District Councils and many local people employed getting the camp ready for the first holiday visitors. The holiday with pay schemes had started and promoted by the Daily Express. The camp had 1100 chalets, a twenty metre tower, an exquisite dance hall and a dining hall that was serviced with waitresses.

15th July – the camp was opened on the Saturday, dance bands and Eddie Phillips was the singer and crooner as they were called then. Eddie Phillips was a Light Heavy Weight Champion Boxer and was welcomed at Prestatyn Railway Station by Councillor Norman Stewart. Eddie arrived on the `Welshman` train, first stop in Prestatyn from Euston, London. I mention the holiday camp as possible trade for the Scala.

8th July - `The Four Feathers` with Ralph Richardson and C Aubrey Smith and June du Pre.

8th July – complaints about the Speedway in Bastion Road being noisy.

17th July – Emlyn Williams' `They Dream at Night` in which he starred.

19th July – the Siren was tested in Prestatyn.

26th August – Gracie Fields in `Shipyard Sally`.

On one occasion before the war, she came to perform at the Rhyl Pavilion and there were too many people to be seated inside. So they had to put loud speakers outside for people to be able to enjoy her performance.

26th August – Councillor Mrs Eleanor Evans, Chair of PUDC, with the threat of war, asked for calmness, confidence and faith.

2nd September – Prestatyn.

840 evacuees arrive, mostly children. People who took them in, a child was 10/6d (52p) two children 17/- (85p), mothers 5/- (25p) and for each child with their mother 3/- each. These charges were per week.

4th September – War was declared about 11am. Sirens sounded everywhere. The camp soldiers started to move two weeks before war was declared and the holiday camp was not re-opened to the public for about a year after war ended. The Royal Corps of Signals were the first ones in. Their wives and children soon followed and there was soon very little rooms left for the real evacuees. Prestatyn was never the same again. Many never left the area. Blackouts and bans on torches in the streets. ARP chasing people showing lights. Cars had special fittings on their lamps and also the local Territorials were called up fourteen days before war was declared. After war was declared, I remember being detailed with twenty others to patrol the beach in Rhyl. So we were each given a pick handle, no pick, and if the Germans landed, we were supposed to hit them on the head. The situation was pathetic. We could not see each other so we shouted to keep in touch so the Sergeant Major came onto the prom to tell us to shut up and look for Germans landing. It was pitch black. Talk about heroes lead by donkeys. It was never so true. Most of the officers were bank clerks, accountants and teachers with shiny bottom suits. Lady Astor stood up in Parliament and demanded all soldiers under 18 years of age should not go to France. So all of us under 18 years of age (about 60 of us) were transferred to an anti- aircraft unit. 60 of us went to Newcastle-on Tyne. I was on guard with a rifle. An officer came up and said he wanted my rifle for the LDV (Local Defence Volunteers). I was given a Vicars Phosphorous Bomb in replacement. It was a glass pop bottle about 7" high by 2" diameter full of phosphorous which I was supposed to throw at a German if I saw one. I carried it in my pocket. If someone had hit it and broken it, I would have been incinerated. I was 17 years old. I am not aware of drastic changes in the Scala after war started and there was just picture after picture at the Scala till 1963.

During this time, one of the projectionists Glyn Jones, now 90 years old. Bill posting was one of his jobs from Dyserth to Ffynnongroew, with a bucket of past and a brush and advertising of the Scala films. Glyn told be that when the paper upon the billboard became thick, they would slide the sheets off with a spade. Bunny Scratch Edwards would buy a bucket of tar from the gasworks and apply it to a sheet of thick paper and put it on the roof of his shed to waterproof it to protect his animals.

Mr Saronie pre war had an American car. It was a large blue Essex saloon. After the war started all large cars were confiscated, bodies removed and fitted with a simple ambulance body and presented to the ARP. So Mr Saronie lost his car, his pride and joy.

After WW2, Mr Saronie bought a Bristol car, built by the Bristol Aircraft Co. It was metallic blue and was a crowd puller wherever it stopped. Mr Price of Meliden was his chauffeur and handyman.

1940.

21st September 1940, it was reported in the Prestatyn Weekly that WVS gave shoes and clothing and shelter supplied by the town to over fifty men, women and children who had lost everything in bombing raids in England.

1st January 1940, there was an early train to Rock Ferry, return fare 1 /6 (which is equal to 7.5p today). All sorts of people used the service, shopping in Liverpool, evacuees going home for the day.

13th January Lord Mostyn`s son was shot in Glasgow. He and his friends were playing with a loaded gun.

28th January, sugar, butter and bacon became rationed.

5th February, the film `Stanley and Livingston.` with Spencer Tracey and Cedric Hardwicke, Nancy Kelly and Richard Green. No torches to be used in the street. The Warren at Talacre was a major area of exposed torches and lots of fines of £2.

Lady Reading stated that the Welsh WVS were first rate.

30th March 1940, WVS demonstration of War Time Cooking at 33 High Street, Prestatyn. The PUDC supplied the equipment.

20th March, an annual meeting of the WRV, a remarkable record of the work at the Scala Canteen.

25th May, 500 soldiers per day were being served.

13th July, Mr Saronie allowed the WVS to collect aluminium saucepans and kettles to be processed to make aeroplanes. They were collected at the Arcadia Gardens which he owned.

Advice to keeping chickens. 4 hens can produce 3 eggs daily.

It was decided that people could eat in cafes without coupons, thus the Palladium Café and Aunt Jane`s were always full. Oh to be rich. You had to pay 5/- and no more.

If you don`t like margarine beat in an egg. It was said to taste like butter.

People were allowed preserving sugar, 3 lb (1.5 K) and 1lb of oranges from Seville to make marmalade.

As rationing became more serious, sugar was sold in 12 oz packets.

20th July – Paul Robeson in `Proud Valley.`

21st September – Shirley Temple in `Bluebird.`

1941.

5th April, Lady Reading visits Prestatyn WVS and approves of all the work that is being done to help the plight of refugees who are homeless due to bombing raids. They provide food and clothes and organise the shelter for these distraught people by the hundreds.

Mr Atlee`s Labour Government gave financial help to the WVS.

16th April, Lord and Lady Stamp who brought the Tower Beach Camp to Prestatyn were killed in an air raid in London. Lord Stamp and Vincent Smith brought the camp to town. Lord Stamp, GCB, GBE, born in 1880 was an economist of world renown, Director of the Bank of England, Chief Economic Advisor to the government and President of The British Association.

WVS, the Tontine Committee, funded a mobile canteen and presented the unit to the WVS as they would make full use of it.

1 million ladies belonged to the WVS, 420 of whom were in Prestatyn alone, knitting socks for the forces and altering clothes, including adding collars to soldier`s shirts by cutting a piece from the tail of each shirt to make them as smart as the Italian soldiers who always wore collars and ties.

9th August - end of double summertime which was used during the war.

1942.

21st February Mr Saronie was reading the Daily Film Renter. It contained an article by Tatler of the Waldour Street Gossip Group. Tatler said `As I entered the Savoie this morning, I was astounded to see Lloyd George walking towards me. It was Saronie of Liverpool, a dead ringer for Lloyd George. It was a pleasure to meet him.`

22nd March – Harold MacMillan MP, Secretary of State for the Colonies, by permission of Mr Saronie, spoke at the Scala.

30th April – Errol Flynn and Olivier de Haviland in `Santa Fe Trail`.

3rd July – A tribute to the WVS ladies by the County Leader for WVS a Mrs Doris Oates who worked from Mold.

10th August – A Russian Film of how the Russians defeated the enemy at Moscow.

27th October – WVS started a Housewife Section. They repaired socks and clothing for evacuees in their own homes.

28th October – `The Scarlet Pimpernel` with Leslie Howard, Merle Oberon and Raymond Massey.

24th December – Remember Pearl Harbour.

1943.

30th January – Bing Crosby in `The Holiday Inn` in which he sang `I'm Dreaming of a White Christmas`.

6th February – Noel Coward, Celia Johnson, John Mills film `In Which We Serve`.

WVS celebrates 6 years in the Scala Rooms.

17th June - `The Four Feather` with John Clements, Ralph Richardson and June Duprey.

3rd November, - James Cagney in `Yankee Doodle Dandy`.

1944

18th March – Diana Durban in `Hers to Hold`.

1st May – Ronald Coleman and Loretta Young in `Clive of India`.

20th May – Orson Welles and Joan Fontaine in `Jane Eyre`.

19th June – The Tunisian Victory in War News.

9th July – Sunday. The Flintshire Red Cross and St John's Personnel Show for the War Fund. Sergeant Gerald Davies stationed at the camp, was in civilian life a Tenor of the Carla Rosa Co. who performed at Covent Garden, London and Osia Gwyn Ellis was the Harpist.

17th July – Irving Berlin's film `This is the Army Mr Jones`. With Ronald Reagan and the song `This is my English Buddy.`

4th July - `The Desert Song`. Denis Morgan and Irene Mannering.

30th September – Saronie`s Golden Wedding. Prestatyn Weekly stated that he was a prominent Citizen of Birkenhead. He was a founder member of the North West Cinematography Industry and was well known in this industry. His wife was an expert photographer, married St Nicholas Parish Church, Liverpool on 30th September 1894.)

PRESTATYN WEEKLY

Prestatyn Golden Wedding

Photo: H J Lewis, Prestatyn

MR. & MRS. J. R. SARONIE, of Hillcourt, Prestatyn, celebrate their Golden Wedding on Saturday, Sept. 9. Mr Saronie a native of Merseyside, is one of the best known figures in the Cinematograph Industry, being a founder of the North West Area Cinematograph Exhibitors' Association. He has seen great developments in the industry since the days when he was a pioneer of the old Animated Pictures, and as a prominent photographer he used to take the pictures and then screen them.

Before coming to Prestatyn Mr Saronie took a keen interest in Merseyside Civic affairs, and is a former member of Birkenhead Borough Council.

Mrs. Saronie, herself an expert photographer, operated the Studios in Grange Road, Birkenhead, for many years, and also took a keen interest in Civic affairs, being a member of the Ladies' Charity Committee.

Mr. & Mrs. Saronie were married at St Nicholas' Parish Church, Liverpool, on Sept. 30th, 1894.

4th November – a cry out for a public hall.

20th October – Ingrid Bergman in `For whom the bell tolls` with Gary Cooper.

18th November – Bob Hope and Madeline Carroll in `My Favourite Blond`.

6th September – Vera Lynn and Geraldo`s Orchestra in `We`ll Meet Again`.

13th September – Madeline Carroll and Robert Donat in `Thirty Nine Steps`.

17th March – Alexander`s Rag Time Band with Tyrone Power and Alice Fey.

14th September – Anne Ziegler and Webster Booth in `Demobbed`.

17th September – Welcome Home Concert at the Scala with kind permission of Mr Saronie.

23rd December - `The Song of Bernadette` with Jennifer Jones.

1945.

Saronie honoured by the industry. The Prestatyn Weekly ran an article that shows he was a pioneer of the movies.

27th October 1945 the Prestatyn Weekly ran a long and interesting article showing what work the WVS had achieved for the forces during the war.

`Arsenic and Old Lace` with Cary Grant and Raymond Massey as the monster-looking brother.

27th August – Lawrence Olivier in `Henry V`. The real king took 3 million arrows with him to war.

13th October – the passing of John Roberts – stage name Wilford Roberts – the butcher of the High Street, Prestatyn. Bass Baritone, he often sang at the town hall, from Dublin Radio and the North Region, Manchester.

It was reported in the Prestatyn Weekly that Mrs Massey and Mrs Clayton organised the WVS events and also the continuing work that the ladies achieved in mending clothes to be handed out to those in need.

N.B. A Special Accolade to the Ladies of WVS of Prestatyn.

Due to the kindness of Mr J R Saronie, the WVS had their Headquarters at The Scala in the Green Room, worthy of the cause. And the County Leader, Mrs Doris Oates congratulated them. People who had been bombed in the cities of North West England and some from London, arrived in the only clothes they stood up in. Thus gifts handed to them by the towns folk were supplied and accommodation found. Many such cases happened in this predicament.

After six years and three months, the WVS had administered to thousands of soldiers of the Royal Corps of Signals, the Pioneer Corps and the RAF, a `home from home` for them. Making and mending clothes, 45,000 pairs of socks, 5,807 pairs of woollen gloves, 997 pullovers, 57 sets of pyjamas, 2,617 vests and pants, 62 pyjama vests, 530 pairs of shorts, 638 shirts, 48 pairs of denim trousers and 49 army tunics were altered.

A Pioneer of the Movies

INTERESTING REMINISCENCES ON FIFTIETH ANNIVERSARY

When children threw admission money into a fire bucket

The name of Saronie figured, prominently in the recent nation-wide celebration of the fiftieth anniversary of the showing of the "first moving picture" and the primitive beginnings of the cinema business consisting of short films shown in town halls were recalled with interest by many old-film goers,

The early cinema show would be a cause of amazement to the present-day young "film fan" used to luxurious palaces. When Mr J.R. Saronie, Prestatyn. first brought moving films to Birkenhead at the beginning of this century and showed the films he had himself taken of local events at the Coliseum, Tranmere (which lasted about two minutes each) he was indeed regarded as a pioneer of something almost magic. The thirty foot films, after being shown, were rushed by cyclists at break neck speed to his other cinema at the Park, Tranmere, where a show was also in progress.

The show then was interspersed with performances. Among the earliest films taken and shown to a wondering public by Mr. Saronie. were those of the launching of a ship from Messrs Cammell Lairds, Mersey river scenes, soldiers embarking troops-ships, to go to fight in the South African war, scenes on Mafeking day and the visit of the then Prince of Wales (later King Edward VII) to Ruthin.

In those days the children's visit to the cinema was confined to the Saturday matinees or as it became popularly known the penny rush.

To facilitate the entry of the crowds of youngsters, a fire bucket was placed by the entrance, and guarded by the manager. Into this the children threw their penny entrance fee. There was then no entertainment tax.

Mr Saronie brought the first movie to Prestatyn on Monday January 9th 1899, when the first film show in the town was held at the old "British Schools," facing the Coronation gardens. An original poster described the films as "animated photograph". the greatest wonder of the 19th century, The poster stated that the entertainment would include talks, songs and whistles. The various appellations which included "electric films" suggest that the pioneers were searching for the right description and it was many years before the slick terms of "movie" and the "flicks" were found.

Later Mr. Saronie held regular shows at Prestatyn Town Hall, now the "Scala Cinema". In the Prestatyn Weekly of 1913 there was a large "Preliminary announcement" of the "grand reopening of the Town Hall with Saronies world famous electric pictures"

The program was changed twice weekly. Mr Saronie, was then the only, as well as the pioneer cinematographer in North Wales. Later he had cinema shows at Rhyl, Denbigh and Ruthin, during the first world war, at Kinmel for the troops. It was in 1915 that Miss Hardman became Mr Saronies manageress at the Scala and in that post she has discharged her duties towards thousands of cinema goers with great courtesy and efficiency for thirty one years.

In the recent anniversary issue of the "Kinemotograph Weekly" Mr. Saronie is placed among the first and most successful pioneers of the industry and his lifetime as almost the history of cinema itself. At the end of the span of the fifty years progress from the two minutes film to the two hour technicolour in luxurious surroundings he is to be congratulated on his work and enterprise.

from

ABC Prestatyn Weekly

The WVS local Chief Mrs J W Ellis who was also Treasurer and the Chief Canteen orderly Mr Eddie Donachie of Delamere were present for the New Year Party and mention was made of the staunch work of Mrs Massey and Mrs Carlyle. Mrs Massey said thanks for all the praise she and Mrs Carlyle had received. (Mrs Massey went on to run the catering for WVS till she was 98).

5,183,490 cups of tea had accrued 7,167,600 pennies.

The councillors and officials of the town joined in the praise of the ladies who helped to make things easier for the members of the forces and the many people who had lost their homes and possessions in bombing raids in all the major towns in the country.

Various Prestatyn camp commanders also joined in the thanks to the WVS.

450 members of WVS were killed whilst carrying out their volunteer duties during the war due to their ever ready presence in the bombing raids in the large towns in England.

1946.

After 31 years Miss Hardman left Mr Saronie's employment, she was his Manageress, having joined him in 1925 at the Town Hall.

Madam Leila Megane at the Scala 24th February 1946. A concert on behalf on the English Congregational Church, Prestatyn and was to be accompanied by her husband on the piano. T. Osborne Roberts, Mr T J Price-Edwards and Mr Brunt also took part.

6th June - `Brief Encounter` with Celia Johnson and Trevor Howard, a classic film of wartime encounters.

15th July - `The Corn is Green` with Bette Davies. The script was written by Emlyn Williams of Ffynnongroew.

14th September – The History of Prestatyn Urban District Council. The First Chairman in 1896, Town Clerk Mr John Hughes.

7th July - Mr Saronie sells his picture houses in Bangor, The Plaza and The City to the Paramount Pictures. So he is left with the Scala as a hobby I presume.

1947

30th June to 1st July, the WVS, a consignment of Corned Beef from Friends Overseas. The WVS Headquarters at the Scala building, will distribute the tins of meat, one tin per person for the over 70`s over the two days.

1948.

29th May, the WVS negotiate with the PUDC for a site in Kings Avenue.

17th July – the WVS 10th Anniversary was held at St Paul`s Cathedral, London.

23rd December – Royal Command Film - `The Bishop`s Wife` with David

Niven, Loretta Young and Cary Grant.

22nd September - `Forever Amber` with Linda Darnell, Cornell Wilde, George Sanders and Richard Greene.

In October of this year, collecting rose hips. The WVS was the collection point and people were paid 3d per pound or 4 lbs for 5p. They were made into Rose Hip Syrup to help coughs and colds for the vitamin C after many years food deprivation.

14th September – The Irish Mail Train Service was 100 years old. And still carrying the watch to Dublin with Greenwich Mean Time.

14th August, the Welfare Clinic in Kings Avenue was opened.

1st November - `Gone with the Wind`. Clerk Cable, Vivien Leigh, Olivier de Haviland and Lesley Howard, said to be the greatest film ever to be produced.

1949

22nd January, the WVS found a new area of activity, The Derby and Joan Club and held their first Christmas Party at their HQ.

The picture `The Girls in the News` with Margaret Lockwood and Emlyn William

18th September, Professor Laski, Economic Advisor to the Labour Government, by kind permission of Mr Saronie, and the Scala was crammed full that day, gave a lecture on economics. I don`t know what Mr Saronie`s politics were, but he deserved an OBE or MBE for the charities he supported.

1950

24th July – In the minutes of Prestatyn Urban District Council, there was recorded a Gift of Land where Mrs Groome used to keep her caravan (previously mentioned) and now known as Pendre Gardens. The Clerk read a letter from Messrs Clement Hughes and Co., Solicitors on behalf of the donors of the above land, i.e. the late Mr J F King, Mr J R Saronie and Mr Clement Hughes, expressing the hope that the gift would help the amenities of the town. The Chairman of the Parks and Amenities Committee, Mrs Eleanor Evans JP referred to the gift as a magnificent one and centrally situated. She said that it (PUDC) proposed to lay out the land in a worthy manner and with that end in view she expressed the hope that the response to the appeal for funds in connection with a War Memorial would be adequate for this purpose.

29th July – the pictures shown on the 50 years Anniversary of the Scala was Betty Grable in `Warbash Avenue` and `Cheaper by the Dozen` with Clifton Webb and Myrna Loy.

```
464.  PENDRE GARDENS - GIFT OF LAND.
        The Clerk read a letter from Messrs. Clement Hughes &
Co., Solicitors, on behalf of the donors of the above land -
the late Mr. James F. King, Mr. J. R. Saronie and Mr. Clement
Hughes - expressing the hope that the gift would help the
amenities of the town.
        The Chairman of the Parks and Amenities Committee (Clr.
Eleanor Evans, J.P.) referred to the gift as a magnificent one
and centrally situated.  She said that it is proposed to lay-out
the land in a worthy manner and, with that end in view, she
expressed the hope that the response to the appeal for funds
in connection with the War Memorial would be adequate for this
Purpose
                        - 137 -
```

(Today Prestatyn Town Council run and maintain Ty Pendre which was the public toilet built as part of this amenity for the original gardens).

Bookings at Chatsworth House on that date were 795. They had recorded 2000 births up to date from when the Vernon Ladies started, when they first organised the maternity equipment in the late thirties.

Liverpool Corporation who had Chatsworth House during the war as a maternity hospital handed the premises over to Dr Tudor Griffiths before the NHS was instigated in 1949.

I never intended this to be a history of Prestatyn, only things connected with the Scala Picture House and the personalities who were involved. So many ladies were usherettes and cleaners that it would be unfair to mention some and not others.

Also many events which helped to evolve the town over fifty years were also connected with the Scala and the residents who were its patrons.

1963

The Scala was taken over by the Prestatyn Urban and District Council at the retirement of Mr Saronie. The council refurbished the theatre and used plastic on the front of the building and like all plastic, looks tacky after twenty years. The shops were included in the takeover. The theatre had a £10,000 grant from the Arts Council to construct the stage with scenery rolls in the ceiling. But these were hardly used with exception by Rev. Clive Southerton and his musical players who used this facility when he put on his musicals. One year we had the Welsh Operatic Society.

The Green Room was an asset but with about twenty five stairs it was impossible for invalids to climb. Exhibitions of all sorts were held there, keep fit classes, etc. Also the display of Richard Wilson`s paintings collected by Mrs

Christo, herself an art teacher. Richard Wilson RA, 1713 – 1782. When Richard was in his late teens, his father was rector of Gwaenysgor, and Richard is accredited with the painting of the original Cross Foxes sign, not the rubbish of later years.

I wonder what happened to the original. It was the logo of the Wynne family and is carved in the wall of Bodelwyddan Castle up Engine Hill.

The Scala was situated in a central position in the centre of the town but some people found the parking of cars difficult.

I hope we have a tourist centre within the building hopefully run like the one in Betws y Coed to assist visitors with overnight B&B. The live theatre could be used for modern Pierrots in the summer as Saronie had whilst he was in the Palladium and the Arcadia Gardens at the top of the High Street.

The stories and tales I have heard that are connected with Saronie, his customers and associates. Miss Hardman and Mr Sanderson were the managers and the latter operator of the projectors.

We also used to have a film company in Prestatyn called "Parker Film Distributors" they were based in the out buildings in Bryntirion House, on Melidan Road. The van driver worked all night and on Wednesdays, delivering and collecting films, he covered Holyhead, Amlwch, Dolgellau, Wrexham and South Flintshire and of course "The Scala". I remember one of the drivers was called Bill Otley.

So I conclude my brief history of the Scala. It has been rewarding in the information I have gathered about local affairs and the WVS in particular that Mr Saronie gave his full support to. I hope you enjoy the gleanings of fifty years of the history of the Scala Theatre / Cinema.

1997.

The Fall and Rise of the Scala.

Due to developers being allowed to pump thousands of gallons of water out of the marsh land which I named earlier Cwr y Traeth, to enable to build over 200 houses at Ffordd Parc Bodnant, the water table fell from High Street to Bodnant Bridge. And the consequences were that buildings lost their support and started to crack and distort, and the Scala seemed to be the one most affected so it became unsafe for public use.

Over the years, The Scala was inspected annually for safety. First by local builders or persons of that trade, then came the County Health Officer and the inspection covered structure, doors, seats, carpets, toilets and fire curtains. And that is how it came to be condemned and closed.

Alas it was to be eliminated to be a shopping arcade, entrance to the new Tesco Supermarket and all sorts of ideas floated in the air.

Mrs Sandra Pitt gathered together a few friends, formed a committee called `The Friends of the Scala` and kept the idea of a new theatre in the public eye for 8 years. She collected 5000 signatures in two days. This was handed to Denbighshire County Council and as a result, action was taken and we have under construction a Community Centre with restored frontage much like the original 108 years ago.

And so my story ends of the "Town Hall to the Scala".

I have enjoyed the the effort, I've gained a lot of knowledge and met a lot of new interesting people.

So I give this book to "Friends of the Scala" to help them with their fundraising.   *Fred Hobbs 2009*

Saronie at retirement in 1963

Chapter 6 - Looking Back
- *Seventeen Years with the Saronies.*

by Mrs Vivien Hughes-Davies

One day in 1928, Nain Davies who lived on Mostyn Road in Lower Gronant, had a visitor. It was Mrs Saronie. Nain's grand-daughter has been in service for Mrs Saronie in Birkenhead where Mr Saronie had a cinema until Sally left to get married. Mrs Saronie enquired if Nain knew of a good, clean girl who she could employ as a living-in domestic and companion. Grace Mary Price next door was at the school leaving age of fourteen. Her future was arranged at a starting wage of eight shillings (40p) per week. Grace's parents were a little dubious, thinking she would fret about leaving the family home.

"We will be your Dad and Mam now." Said Mr and Mrs Saronie. Grace was to stay with them for seventeen years.

Mr Saronie whose actual name was James Roberts, was born in Liverpool in 1872, the son of Captain Roberts of the SS `Great Eastern` who is buried in Prestatyn Churchyard. Young Jim Roberts used to come to Prestatyn with his mother for months at a time when Captain Roberts was away at sea. They stayed at a cottage where Carson's shop is at the top of Prestatyn's High Street. Not to miss out on his education, Jim attended the National School.

Mr Saronie was married at twenty one to an eighteen year old girl from South Wales. Their mutual interest was photography. Her earliest assignment was to take photos of Harry Lauder for publicity purposes. Mr Saronie was a professional photographer in his early days and was pleased to have been called in to take photographs of Edward VII when he came to visit Ruthin Castle for a shooting party and other attractions.

There was no snobbishness or upstairs-downstairs atmosphere at Hillcourt, the Saronie home in Prestatyn.It stood high above the town near a well-known landmark, i.e.. The house with the green domes observatory that was the holiday home of a Warrington family called Thorpe. Grace's work was hard by present day standards but there was no harassment. She was not required to wear a uniform and ate at the same table as her employers. Their tastes in food were simple. One favourite was `jobbins maip` which was potatoes mashed with turnip and butter, pickled red cabbage and slices of gammon taken from hams and joints of bacon that were hung in the cool basement and these came from the farm of Mrs Saronie's`s family. No refrigerator there but gas and electricity were both laid on in the house.

Grace remembers the large stone fireplaces in the dining room and lounge, the one of Gwespyr Stone, the other of Prestatyn limestone, both built by Grace`s uncle, Bob Price. When Mr Saronie was away on one of his business trips, his wife and Grace would sit in the `den` with a bright fire in the red tile grate that was so much easier to keep clean than the stone fireplaces with hearths that had to be `donkey-stoned`. These fireplaces were furnished with copper fire irons and polished steel firedogs and edged with heavily engraved kerbs.

The floors in some rooms were wood block and in others polished wood strip overlaid with red Indian carpets which had to brushed by hand with dustpan and brush. They would be taken outside annually for a thorough beating on the back lawn by the chauffeur. No vacuum cleaners then.

At that time the curtains which were cretonne or tweedy folk weave would also be taken down and washed in the `dolly tub`. White sheets and other linen had to be boiled weekly and was blued and starched and carefully ironed using flat irons heated on the gas stove. There was always plenty of hot water from the central heating boiler in the cellar where there were lines for hanging clothes on to dry if the weather was inclement.

At Spring Cleaning time, more help was brought in to cope with the extra work and Grace was at liberty to choose helpers that she knew personally as good workers like her own mother. Washing up was done after meals using scraps of Sunlight Soap in a wire device that was shaken in the water to set up a good lather with washing soda added of there were greasy utensils to be washed. This did not contribute towards soft ladylike hands. The silver was cleaned with Goddards Silver Powder and methylated spirits.

On one memorable occasion Mr Saronie`s sometimes uncertain temper got the better of his overlay of gentlemanliness. He strode red faced towards the dining room where his porridge awaited his attentions, picked up the bowl and hurled it and contents across the room. It so happened that all the newly cleaned silver was on the sideboard awaiting madam`s approval to be put away. It became generously garnished with the glutinous cereal. He strode off while the round-eyed young Grace faced the task of re-polishing it all. She was relieved to be told that a wash in soapy water would suffice and to take no notice of Sir`s paddies as he had a lot on his mind. He would sometimes tell robust jokes which Grace found a bit rude but his conduct towards the girl was never offensive. She was always treated with great kindness.

In some rooms the walls were panelled in oak inlaid with diamond shaped motifs in black and amber. Grace was instructed not to apply polish but to rub the wood with vinegar and water in order to preserve its character. The polishing of floors, like the brushing of carpets and stairs, was a hand knees job. The doors were made from wood from the old Town Hall which Mr Saronie had bought to convert into a cinema that he called the `Scala` and the furniture was custom made in Birkenhead to Mr Saronie`s specification, some of which inlaid with copper decoration and the dining room chairs with pigskin seats.

While Grace did the morning chores, Mrs Saronie would don a pair of trousers and slip on a pair of clogs to go out into the garden. They employed a gardener but she liked to attend to the finer horticultural points herself. It was certainly not an easy garden to tackle since the front approach was up what Grace thinks were fifty steps. In a cavity in one of the terracing retaining walls, Mrs Saronie inserted for posterity, a collection of current newspapers. When Grace rang a little bell for morning coffee, madam would come, clean up, drink up and get changed to go shopping in town, walking down to the shops with her basket.

Little entertaining was done by the Saronie household and it could be described as non-smoking and tee-total except for medicinal purposes. The whiskey and gin were kept for use to treat colds: a hot toddy worked wonders and the gin was used to alleviate female disorders. There was an occasional family gathering when a goose from South Wales appeared on the table when there was an indulgence for a toast. Grace never forgot that her father was told to go from the Top Chapel in Gronant, Calvinistic Methodist because someone saw him standing outside a pub in Rhyl and told the minister. The Rev. and elders refused to listen to his reason that he had waited outside for his mates inside. He was found guilty by association so he joined the Wesleyans in the Bottom Chapel.

A Christmas guest at Hillcourt was Mrs Groom, called by some locals the Queen of the Gypsies, a genuine Romany. She was black haired even in her old age, had piercing dark eyes in her brown wrinkled face, had sparkling gold rings and ear rings and always dressed in black. She lived in a traditional gypsy caravan beneath the Holm Oak opposite the Cross Foxes Pub and behind what used to be Pendre Farm. There is now a small public garden tended by Prestatyn Town Council and Prestatyn Horticultural Society and Ty Pendre Hall which used to be the toilets. After Mrs Groom had eaten her lunch, she would then tell the fortunes of the others to repay their hospitality. When she died, her caravan was burnt and it is said that Pat Collins, Showman, paid for her funeral expenses. The service at Rhyl`s St Thomas`s Church was attended by crowds including many gypsy folk. And she was buried in Rhyl cemetery. Previous to living in Prestatyn, she had lived for many years on the estate of the old Duke of Westminster near Chester. Mrs Groom left five cats which were not incinerated with her other possessions but were adopted by Mr Saronie who built a shed to accommodate them.

During the evenings when Mr Saronie was away on his business trips Mrs Saronie would tell Grace of the assignments she and her husband had been on and of her his plans to open a Cinema in Bangor. She was an entertaining raconteur while Grace listened as she did her embroidery. Mrs Saronie`s needlework talents were used for creating glamourous nightgowns, petticoats and French knickers.

The Saronies home, Hillcourt, Prestatyn.

When War was declared, she was afraid that Grace would be called on to carry out War Work so she arranged that two airmen from the base on a high point of the hill behind the house should be billeted with them. Thus Grace could be classified as doing essential work.

Grace remembers well when Mr Saronie opened his two cinemas in Bangor, `The Plaza` and `The City.`

`The Plaza` was at first a wooden building which was taken down later and presented for use as a community centre site. When built, the Plaza was opened by the then Prince of Wales, later to become the uncrowned Edward VIII, and this was followed by a Hot Pot Supper. When the newly built Plaza opened, David Lloyd George was present with Dame Margaret and their daughter Lady Carey Evans. On this occasion, Mr Saronie stayed at the British Hotel nearby. Grace stayed at Llanllechid with a cousin and they were invited to the First Night which was a showing of `Little Women`. They were shown upstairs to balcony seats by an usherette and presented with a box of chocolates with Mr and Mrs Saronie`s compliments. After the show, they enjoyed a complimentary meal at the British Hoel. Another early film was one staring Al Jolson.

Grace continued her work at Hillcourt after her marriage since her husband was overseas in the forces. She says that at her wedding at Bethel Chapel in Gronant, she proudly wore real pearls belonging to Mrs Saronie. Something borrowed.

Mr and Mrs Saronie celebrated their Golden Wedding by going on a trip to Australia via America. They wanted Grace to go along with them but by this time, Grace was expecting a baby so she missed that three month long treat. She stayed on at Hillcourt to look after the property in their absence.

Some time later, Grace`s mother had a stroke and she had to take temporary leave of what had become her home. The old lady made little progress and some three months later, a further blow fell when Grace met Mrs Saronie in Prestatyn who told her abruptly to collect her possessions from Hillcourt since a replacement domestic had been found. It was the only time she had received anything but kindness from her employers. Mrs Saronie apologised some time later and demonstrated her goodwill on several occasions in a practical manner. Grace`s children also benefited from free tickets to Saronie`s enterprises at the Scala Cinema.

Many will remember him either sitting upstairs in the balcony at every performance making sure that couples sitting in the double seats did no more than discreetly hold hands. Or he sat in the back row downstairs ready to eject any youngsters he spotted misbehaving. He told those watching nearby what was coming next in the film.

His white Lloyd George haircut and pomaded pointed moustache were well know in the town, but wearing an artist`s beret he would often be seen painting local views at his easel. An old post card of Coed Bell shows him near a fallen Rown at bluebell time, painting away. Many of his paintings were stacked away in Hillcourt attic.

Grace asked Mrs Saronie once where that name came from because she had been told their name was really Roberts. They said that, like film stars, some names sound more distinguished than others and that at that time, names that sounded Italianate or foreign names for people or places of entertainment were in vogue. Thinking on that, Grace could not but agree that Saronie`s Scala sounded more upper crust than Roberts` Cinematograph. Mrs Saronie also confided that her brother, a photographer whose surname was Thomas, adopted the name Vanderbilt which gave his clients more confidence in his abilities.

James Roberts, Mr Saronie, was a shrewd business man, elevating from a photographer to the owner of several cinemas; two in Birkenhead, one called the Coliseum which had been a variety theatre and assembly rooms. This he converted to his first cinema, later bought by Essoldo, closed in 1963. And the other was a skating rink which became the City Electric Cinema. He also had two cinemas in Bangor, one called the Plaza and the other called the City. He had a theatre in Kinmel Camp for the troops during WWI and in Prestatyn he had the Scala, the Palladium for 7 years and the Arcadia Gardens at the top of the High Street for Live Entertainment. And there may have been others.

The Saronies circa 1915

Chapter 7 - From start to finish
- 'The show must go on'

We've decided to start with a bit of a time line of the history of the Scala from closure to present day. During December 2000 the last few days of a much loved cinema play out. Walls with no plaster that had been painted to help make them look better, a balcony long since disused, condemned and sealed off to the public. Paint was peeling, the state of repair appalling despite maintenance by the staff who loved working there and everyone was devastated when it closed.

For most people today the thought of visiting the cinema conjures up a trip out of town to a metal structure in a retail park. For the people of a busy tourist town on the North Wales coast and for the thousands of regular tourists to Prestatyn and local residents, "The Scala" was the traditional cinema experience surviving even more elegant cinemas of the town's yesteryear.

In December 2000 the last film shown was Jim Carey in *The Grinch*, a Christmas tale, with an all-star cast.

Friends of the Scala with a few dedicated members of staff and friends began to get the cogs turning. Growing in numbers with people concerned and interested to do their best to keep the Scala alive, the Friends grew from strength to strength arranging meetings and deciding what to do and how to do it. We became a constituted group.

In February 2001 a public meeting was advertised and held by Denbighshire County Council at the Nova centre. We were absolutely amazed. If we were to say that the seating arrangements were seriously underestimated at the Starlight Suite it would be an understatement. We had to get the white plastic chairs in from outside, and even then there were people sitting on the tables and quite a few standing. We were so pleased that over 400 people of our little town flocked to give their support.

At the meeting many questions were asked of Town and County councillors. It was agreed that there was a demand for the building to stay open to be refurbished. The Scala Advisory Group was set up to oversee and act as a sounding board to steer the project on its way. The Advisory Group, organised and run by Denbighshire being set up with key members of the community, including Sandra Pitt, Chairperson for the Friends of the Scala and other keen members of FoS.

In March 2001 Friends of the Scala was officially born forming a proper group of people to lobby the council for this much loved and previously well used building to be re-opened.

The first meeting of the Scala Advisory group was held and the Arts Council for Wales awarded a lottery grant for the feasibility study to be done on the Scala building and business as a whole.

May 2001 was a distressing time for The Friends as further deterioration of the Scala's structural condition was discovered. Arches holding up the roof which previously had break glasses fitted to them to watch for movement had cracked showing the building had moved some more on its foundations and the arches designed to hold up the heavy roof were struggling with their job.

External scaffolding was erected to support the roof over the front and main auditorium, floor boards were pulled up so the ground around the main support columns could be excavated, showing that they were not on foundations deep enough to begin with and after the replacing of slate tiles by concrete ones on the roof during the 1960`s was causing the building supports to work even harder to hold the cinema up.

The staff will remember this time the most after months of clearing the building and cataloguing all the items for an inventory, years of memories and show scenery, also unscrewing every chair from the auditorium to be collected. When the Friends and the press were invited to have one final look before the building was demolished, I remember standing on the stage and looking up towards the double doors at the back of the auditorium, now just a hollow empty room and thinking all the life and soul of the building had been drained away. The corridors that had taken people to the foyers and the rest rooms had had the ceilings caved in, the light fittings hanging, it was heart breaking to see a building that was once full of life dead and derelict, hard to believe that just over a year earlier this building was up and running and very much alive, now looking neglected, unused and been decaying for years.

July 2001 and the condition of the building's structure continued rapidly to deteriorate and the decision to demolish the auditorium part of the building was made. I remember taking pictures of the ground space where the auditorium once stood from the exit way of the green room and seeing one last thing that was forgotten when clearing the building, something that I remember being there for years hung on the back wall of the stage. A blue and silver glittery horseshoe which was about five foot across and part of the stage set for the indoor circus that once played at the Scala.

A "draft vision" document was agreed by the Council and the Scala Advisory group. It was published for comment and the consultation document drawn up by Sue Todd and Ron Inglis and presented to the following second public meeting to collect the comments and chosen option by members of the public who although they preferred the Scala as before, were happy to select the idea for both a permanent cinema and also for a live theatre area. The advisory group and friends of the Scala worked closely with the locals trying to keep up local support.

It was then decided to do a feasibility study and funding for the new project was sought.

In December 2002 a very exciting time for us as the new cinema plans were revealed with twin screen designed by Burrell Foley Fischer, based in London and with a lot of experience in designing arts centres, theatres and cinemas.

A community room, studio for Theatre use, visual arts gallery, café bar and improved access were all included.

January 2003 The advisory group unanimously agreed to set up a charitable company to manage and oversee the new Scala. The second more detailed study was completed costing in the region of £50,000 to look at how much potential profit could the Scala business make after opening. In October 2004 the Welsh assembly government awarded the Scala a cash boost to Denbighshire county council of £200,000. October 2005 a long running campaign had been boosted by the Welsh assembly offer of a £1.5 m grant from the physical regeneration fund. This was offered to Denbighshire County Council. The total cost of full regeneration being estimated at approx. £3.5 m at the time.

May 2006 and Denbighshire issued a statement saying they were moving forward with the next phase of four major projects in the county including the Scala. Councillor Paul Marfleet, the lead member for finance said "the Scala Arts Centre plays a pivotal role in the regeneration of the Town" but on19th September 2006 Denbighshire issued a press release stating that the residents of Prestatyn had been given two months to prove they could make the new Scala work as a community project. Denbighshire gave Prestatyn Town Council and the people of Prestatyn until November to prove that they could forward this project. Pending that decision, the allocation previously made to the project be moved elsewhere. This decision came following a thorough debate on the capital plan in which nearly twenty members spoke and resulted in a unanimous decision. Not happy with the way this had been done in October 2006 Friends of the Scala set about hand delivering voting forms asking the people from all residential properties to vote yes or no towards the regeneration to the Scala and how this would benefit the regeneration of Prestatyn town centre. The staggering 5,000 yes votes for the cinema were collected. In November Ann Jones AM handed copies of these voting forms to Edwina Heart at the Welsh assembly. It was also the month of November 2006 that Friends of the Scala officially launched their new website to generate support and interest in the project.

(see "http://www.prestatyn-scala.info")

November 2006 at a meeting in private, Prestatyn Town Council pledged £1.1 m towards the new Scala. This move depended on Denbighshire County at a crucial meeting on the 21st to choose to back the project costing then £3.4 million.

`   If they chose not to back this crucial project the £1.5 m promised by the Welsh assembly would be lost. This was also the month in which Friends of the Scala officially became a registered charity opening up the chances of getting better funding opportunities and to prove that we were here for the long haul. On the 21st November 2006, after considering all the support for the new Scala build, Denbighshire voted yes to the new venue going ahead at the cabinet meeting. All the years of campaigning and fighting for people's support had paid off. A list of councillors who had voted yes or no was obtained by Friends of the Scala.

In Ann Jones' letter to Fred Hobbs, 22nd November 2006 she stated ......"the viability of this project has been threatened but Denbighshire Council's unwillingness to commit to the project the £1.88 million which their plans and bids to the Assembly and other funding bodies originally envisaged. ....have now agreed to contribute £376,000 conditional on Prestatyn Town Council raising £1.1m........which would appear to call into question the basis behind the original Assembly grant offer of £1.5m.......since this is of vital importance to the regeneration of Prestatyn......I will continue to work with the Friends of the Scala and you as residents to see this project realised."

In January 2007 Denbighshire confirmed that all funding was in place and that work would start in March 2007. R L Davies was the successful contractor and David Bellfield said he was delighted to have been chosen to rebuild the Scala facility which he understood how much it meant to the people of Prestatyn.

Friends of the Scala have seen some good fundraising events such as the Scala Gala at Nant Hall Hotel when the rain came down, and it did rain! The fairground rides, stalls and games were all installed. When we were all exhausted with the weather, local councillor Sophia Drew came to help but first bought a second hand coat from a stall and stayed to help for the whole day. It was all worth it as people from Prestatyn and surrounding area flocked in. The day was a huge success and everyone supported our cause. We were glad there was a welcoming bar at the hotel for keeping us warm, for medicinal purposes, of course.

Another great day in the Friends past was the Scala Karaoke challenge, where the friends had an open sided Truck as a stage and were charging people to come up and sing to win the prize money. This was all made possible because Paula from AB-FAB karaoke gave up her free time to support us. I think the only time people stopped singing was to help the vicar Canon Clive Southerton with his world record attempt at the biggest Mexican wave. Another hectic day for all the Friends.

Another huge fundraising venture was 'The Shop'. We took over vacant premises next door to the Scala for a few weeks in 2006 and during this time we raised over £3,000. The local residents scoured lofts and garages, emptied children's play boxes, their own wardrobes were robbed and all in the good cause to raise money to spend on the Scala next door when it reopened. Frank and Lilian Bailey broke all records when it was their day to work in the shop and I have to hank all those who gave their time to help serve and re-stock, tidy up and eventually clear the premises. We all enjoyed running the shop, and meeting the many lovely people of the town, but like a lot of shops in the town we did have our shoplifters, Frank was on duty when we had three watches stolen, he was most upset, but the thing that got him most was the rubber cheque we received, not only did we lose the item but it cost us money in the bank when they bounced it. Thank goodness though 99.9% of the people in our little town are honest. It was ever so interesting in the shop because many people came and told us their stories and memories of the Scala in its heyday, one lady Mrs Joan Steel who used to work for Mr Saronie when he ran the place, and is now an active member of the Friends and is working with us to make our dreams come true. We all had mixed feelings when we received the phone call to tell us to close down and be out in three days, there was utter panic, we had to get rid of the stock, which was mainly furniture, bedding books etc, so we had a mega sale, nothing over 50p, we were the busiest we had ever been but we didn't mind at last our new Scala was going to be built. We emptied the shop in the given time, but guess what? Nothing happened, we kept driving past expecting to see work going on, months went by and still nothing happened, we were bitterly disappointed, the people of the town were stopping us and asking when the work was to start, and we couldn't answer them.

Nor did it all run smoothly for the Friends. We did have our setbacks from time to time and the biggest would have been our Halloween extravaganza, plagued from the start with red tape and rules but we kept on trying to get it off the ground. Unfortunately at the last minute some regulations stopped us in our tracks, with less than twenty four hours to go. Sandra contacted local radio and Melanie ran around town putting up posters, letting the people know it had been cancelled. When the time came there were a lot of very upset people looking forward to the show, but it was out of our hands and a very stressful time for us all; a sad day.

The Prestatyn Carnival has played a big role in the life of Friends of the Scala being one of the best crowd pullers for us to advertise our cause to passing tourists and the ever important residents of Prestatyn. Our carnival floats were always in keeping with the mayors theme but with that added touch to keep the Scala cinema and film element there. To name a few we had the Scala fashion police float, nursery rhymes, the golden age of the silver screen and last year recycling (Recycled Teenagers - High School Musical). All have won prizes in the carnival from 1st place to runner up. We are extremely proud of our achievements in the carnival parade and will continue to support the Prestatyn carnival. We would like to give thanks to Rick Thomson from Weld-Tec for letting us use his pick-up one year and Arriva Buses for letting us use their open top bus for "Holiday on the buses", with Stuart (Sally the Sweetshop lady's husband) as our driver. Also Gavin and Barry who kindly dressed as 'Star troopers' at last year's carnival.

Right from the start all of our fundraising efforts have been supported by the people of the town, and one young boy comes to mind, his name is Ashley Jones - Bryan, he organised a sponsored walk from the Ffrith to Rhyl (Mc Donald's, which we are not supposed to know about) and back again, Ashley was accompanied by his sister Lauren and friends Bethan Joyce, Nathan Maitland-Davies, Jack Sharp and Lauren Bone, all from Penmorfa school, it was wonderful to watch the dedication of this young boy and his friends.

Another youngster that comes to mind, and one none of us will ever be able to forget, is Antonio Jacovelli. This young man designed our logo, his design was chosen from a selection, selected by the teacher at Prestatyn High School, I know he and his family are so proud of him, his design is on our T shirts, the Banner and all our correspondence. The runners up in this competition were Jonathan Harper and Katrina Young, it was such a hard task deciding whose was the best design, it took about ten of us days to decide, all the youngsters had put so much effort in.

When it comes to dedication, it will take a lot to beat Pat Smith who won two free tickets to watch a film at the Scala, unfortunately the Scala was closed before she had time to use them, she had so much confidence in the Friends and the town council she decided to store her prize in a safe place, even though her husband said it would not open in his life time, eight years later she proved him wrong and proudly produced her tickets, at the box office and on Friday 13th 2009 eight years later, her prize was honoured.

Over the years we have seen many changes with Prestatyn Town and County Councillors but have kept up the fight to keep the Scala alive and it has not been easy to say the least. We have had some good and bad confrontations for what we believe should and could happen, but thankfully are still here to tell the tale. The biggest success of all is the new building we see before us now waiting to have the last finishing touches put in. As opening looms people are excited about the new Scala and what it will have in store for the people and holiday makers of Prestatyn.

The new Scala design was a big thing from the start not wanting to get rid of the charm of the building but to make it a more modern and up to date design. The new frontage is a perfect balance of heritage meets modern, with the top half of the façade taken back to its original state matching the terrace surrounding it. The arched windows which are now situated in the Café / Bar area (the old Scala Green room) has taken a lot of work to replace the original façade of Ruabon Brick hidden behind the art deco panelling everyone remembers the Scala for. The lower half of the building has been done in a more contemporary design using glass panels and windows for excellent light to the front of the building. The effect is very apt on Prestatyn's High Street of history enriched buildings.

It does not end here though. Once the new building is re-opened to the public Friends of the Scala will be busying themselves helping out by staffing the Scala on a voluntary basis. This is part of the trusts plan to effectively help with staffing costs and to get the people of Prestatyn and surrounding areas involved with the whole aspect of the building since this is a community orientated building. We hope it becomes the hub of the community like it was before and the reason that made this new venture happen.

I would like to say a big thank you to all involved with Friends of the Scala over the last eight years and to Fred Hobbs for his hours and hours of work put into researching the history for this book.

We did ask the public for their memories, and one lady Connie Brierly who came to Wales 40 years ago, from Lancaster, her memory made me chuckle she tells of how when she visited the Scala, she and her friends would sit on the shabby seats and during the film would find themselves sliding off the seat, she says it was a source of amusement, and probably annoyance to the other people in the cinema. She says how sad she felt when she saw the old girl being demolished, but after many years of hoping it has finally risen again and we can now look forward to a trip to the new Scala in greater comfort, she is so right, the Scala has definitely got the wow!! Factor, and then on the auspicious date of FRIDAY 13th February 2009, the award winning films 'Slumdog Millionaire', 'Bolt' and 'Valkyrie' were the first films to be shown at the 'new' Scala. These are films that we will remember for years to come.

When we decided to write this bit to put in Fred's book, I put an article in the paper asking for peoples memories of the Old Scala, and we were contacted by a few people, it will allow you to get the feel of the old Scala and let you understand how important it has been through the years. Shirley, Joyce Howarth's daughter, contacted us, telling us how her mother used to be an Usherette and towards the end of the 50's became a projectionist whilst under the management of Mr Sanderson, known as "Sandy". Shirley also made herself useful by helping out as a 'Saturday girl' and an ice-cream girl as and when she was needed. This story tells us that the Scala has always been a "family orientated" business. Sadly Joyce passed away in 1999 aged 78.

Melanie Pitt, who worked as a general assistant/projectionist for nearly its last four years, added her memories. She stated it was "the best job she ever had, and ever will". The Scala was at that time, a 300 seat theatre run by 4 staff. Melanie remembers "the regulars", especially a "lovely little old lady who used to get a taxi to the town every night and watch the same film - in the same seat, unaware that she had seen it before".

Another memory of Melanie's was when she went to the projection room to rewind the 'Star Wars' film to find it almost falling out of the projector. As she tried to stop it, it snapped and some film was lost. She apologises to all those who came to see it at the time!

Sian Barker, the Secretary for FOS, who took over from Dan Graham recalled her memories of the Scala when as a youngster (8-10 years old), was sent by her nanna with her brothers, with enough money for a ticket into the "Saturday Matinee" and a packet of Poppet's. She was there every Saturday without fail and wishes that she could do the same for her daughters', Jasmine and Chloe. Last but certainly not least we would like to make a special mention to our members who fought hard with us to save this building over the years, but are sadly no longer with us, Peter Bezodis and Barry Aitken we are sure this building will be a tribute to you both and the hard work and dedication you put in.

Writing this little bit at the end of Fred's book has been an amazing experience, it has been overwhelming the support we have had both financially and emotionally. I would like to thank everyone in "Friends of the Scala" for all their determination and hard work, and the people of the town for their support.

The New Scala is a building to be proud of.

Without *"PEOPLE POWER"* The Town Council etc etc etc we would not have this new facility. I would also like to thank my family for supporting me, because over the past eight years, I know I have neglected them when I have been out fundraising, attending meetings etc.

Sandra Pitt
Chair - Friends of the Scala

Some of our fundraising activities - thank you all.

Clockwise from top left :

Fashion Police - Luke & Colin.
Fred Hobbs as Humpty Dumpty.
Sandra, Glen, Daniel, Sophia and Colin.
Jessica, the youngest member of FoS, as Prom Queen.
Bryn and Stewart.
Melanie as Mary had a little lamb.

THIS BOOK WOULD NOT HAVE BEEN POSSIBLE WITHOUT THE

SUPPORT OF OUR INDIVIDUAL SPONSORS

AS WELL AS LOCAL BUSINESSES.

WE ARE ARE EXTREMELY GRATEFUL TO ALL OF THEM.